Find a Better Way

Retirement Planning for the Best Years of Your Life

Tom Gandolfi

Tom Gandolfi/Three Bridges Financial Group
12725 Morris Road, Suite 130
Alpharetta, GA 30004

www.3bfg.com
Find a Better Way —1st ed.

ISBN 9781660191246

Dedicated to the beautiful women in my family: my mom; my wife, Sherri; and our daughters, Tori and Kasey.

I recently lost my mom after a long, hard battle with cancer. I will always be grateful for her unconditional love, support, and patience. She taught me how to fight for what's right and to love my family.

My wife and our daughters have simply given me the best family that a man could possibly hope for, and this dedication is just another way to express my love.

~Tom

"There's a way to do it better—find it."
—Thomas Edison

TABLE OF CONTENTS

Introduction I

Will I Have Enough Money in Retirement? 1

The Color of Money 9

Managing Risk Factors 21

Creating a Retirement Income Plan 33

Understanding Social Security 45

Filling the Income Gap 63

Accumulation and the Effects of Volatility 73

New Ideas for Investing 79

Taxes and Retirement 91

Different Bridges Cross the Same River: The Roth IRA 105

Your Legacy: A Matter of Dollars and Sense 115

Choosing a Financial Professional 129

About the Author 135

Glossary 137

INTRODUCTION

I'm Tom. I'm not your typical financial advisor. I'm proud of that.

I approach managing money and planning for retirement from a unique angle. I didn't start my business career as a financial services advisor, and I didn't pop out of business school talking about personal finance, mutual funds, ETFs, or corporate bonds.

Instead, after a couple of years in a "corporate" job, I began my career as an entrepreneur. I was the head of my own marketing company that started with three employees: me, myself, and I. I operated and expanded that company for thirteen years as my client list grew, along with demands on my time. Soon I began flying across the country once a week, then twice a week. Eventually I was spending three or four nights each week in a hotel.

In time, my priorities became clear and I realized that watching my kids grow up was more important to me than building my personal empire. So, I sold the company, much to the dismay of my CPA. He kept reminding me of our expansion into nineteen states and our earnings of over $100 million a year in sales. He thought I was making a bad decision, but I was confident in my choice.

So how did I end up as a financial advisor? My journey into personal finance actually began on the other side of the table (as a client) and ultimately led to the writing of this book.

As a business executive, marketing consultant, and owner of a successful company, I made good money and invested a lot of it. I had a broker I liked and trusted from a globally renowned firm, who was considered one of the best. For much of the 1990s, my investments did well, just as I suspect many of your investments did during that timeframe.

Then came 2001. The turn of the century arrived with great hope for a prosperous market. I suspect you know where I'm going with this...

You guessed it. The now notorious "dot-com bubble" burst, and my investments lost hundreds of thousands in market value. Years of hard work squandered in only eighteen months.

I ended up losing more than just money. I lost confidence in the system and the broker I was paying. Based on conversations with him about my risk tolerance and financial goals, I felt like my losses should have been smaller—even in a very difficult market environment, but he didn't really listen to what was important to me.

Ultimately, I blame myself. I was so busy running my business that I failed to realize the high level of risk to which I was exposed. I assumed because I was working with a financial professional described as his company's best, I might have an investment portfolio consistent with my stated goals, with some kind of protection. When the market downturn became a full-scale plunge, any illusions I had were stripped away.

I decided there had to be "a better way" to manage money, and pledged to myself that this would never happen again. I researched, studied, and learned how to effectively manage investments and establish financial goals. Ultimately, I decided to share what I had learned by becoming a financial advisor and eventually wrote this book.

I DID IT MY WAY

From that time on, I made it my life's mission to manage money in more reliable ways. After more than three decades in the business community, I developed a philosophy with accompanying strategies. This, I believe, makes me a better steward of my own money and, more importantly, the money of my clients.

There is nothing new or revolutionary about my approach to money management and retirement planning. I'm not an analog inhabitant of a digital world, nor am I a proponent of "new-age" investing. Rather, I take a "back to the future" philosophy that emphasizes growing wealth and producing income the way American entrepreneurs have for centuries.

Let me explain that in capsule form.

I believe an investor today, especially one nearing or in retirement, must have a solid foundation of predictable income streams from revenue-

producing vehicles (income to supplement Social Security and pensions) in order to become a better, more confident investor.

Put another way, a foundation of sustainable income gives one the ability to resist panicked investment decisions during market downturns (such as the dot-com bubble burst and the Great Recession that followed). Such panic-driven decisions are common during economic downturns and are often catastrophic to one's wealth or retirement savings.

In the upcoming chapters, we'll examine ways to generate these sustained income streams. We'll also examine how this foundation supports the growth of wealth for future retirement needs.

A HISTORICAL PERSPECTIVE

First, let's look at this approach from a historical perspective.

Wealth in our country was once accumulated primarily through investment vehicles. Foremost were stocks and bonds that offered potential for growth (as well as loss) in value and income through dividends and interest.

Today we have even more income-producing investments than were available to the Vanderbilts and Rockefellers of another time. (We will mention those additional options elsewhere in this book.)

But the investment world has changed in ways beyond just new investment vehicles. Investors today don't have to be railroad tycoons, oil barons, or people of great wealth.

Beginning with the explosive growth of the internet in the 1980s, more individual investors from all economic walks of life became involved in market-driven investments. The 1980s were a prelude to the roaring nineties, when the stock market was on fire. In fact, the nineties may have been the best stock market era we will ever experience. There was amazing growth, especially in the technology sector with the development of internet-related startups.

During this time, people did what they often do as part of human nature. They became greedy. They grew accustomed to seeing 20 percent investment returns and believed this was the new normal. Suddenly, a traditional 5.5 percent dividend wasn't as attractive. The psychological bar for investors became much higher than the one used to build wealth in the past. Everyone wanted the quick buck.

That bubble burst in the year 2001 and the downturn continued into 2002. By the time the dust settled, trillions of dollars of stock market shares were lost, and with them the hopes, dreams, and retirement plans for millions of American families. It happened in part because investors realized there wasn't much substance in the highly speculative bets they were making on internet startups. Too many fledgling companies sold more promise and potential than actual production, only to see their stock prices shoot up dramatically before being shot down just as quickly. Consequently, many people experienced dramatic losses in their technology-heavy investment portfolios. I was among them.

WHY I THINK OUTSIDE THE BOX

When I transitioned from private company owner to financial advisor and Investment Adviser Representative, I began to look at innovative approaches to the financial services field.

In starting and growing my marketing company, I had the freedom to be creative and do things differently from my competitors. I continually looked at different options, alternative solutions, and new ways of thinking. I carefully watched what others were doing, and I worked hard to learn everything I needed to know to make informed decisions. I was determined to find a better way to run my company and serve my clients.

My marketing business expanded, not because of any one particular marketing strategy or product, but because of an open mind, option consideration, ignorance of hype, and informed decisions that helped achieve concrete goals.

I brought this same approach to Three Bridges Financial Group, my Atlanta-area financial services company. After years of employing it, I came to the wealth management and retirement planning philosophy I have today, and that is to simply find a better way.

There is a lyric from songwriter Peter Allen that tells us "everything old is new again." I tend to believe that. It's why I've come to appreciate the so-called "old-fashioned way" of making money. This approach is particularly applicable to retirement planning, when an investor may not have time to recover from investment mistakes such as those I made as a younger man.

A CASE STUDY

To illustrate the effect of investment decisions made just before or in the first years of retirement, let's consider a true story involving the father of a long-time buddy of mine.

This gentleman had been a corporate executive at several big companies throughout his long career. As you might imagine, he made a very good income during his working years.

He was not, however, the most financially savvy guy.

He was very intelligent, but not too interested in the stock market or investments. To his credit, he had saved for retirement by investing the maximum amount allowed annually into his company's 401(k) plan. With his company's matching contribution, he believed he would have plenty of money to retire comfortably.

The 401(k) account was the entirety of his retirement plan, but he could not access funds in this account before retiring, with little control over fees, investment vehicles, and fund management.

He had planned to retire in 2009. One of his main goals was to buy a beach house in Florida as a legacy for his family. But in 2008, when the market experienced the major plunge that opened the door for what we now call the Great Recession, purchasing the beach house was no longer a possibility. His retirement dream was gone, along with a huge portion of his 401(k).

Thankfully, my friend's father was still able to live well in retirement on what remained of his savings, but he wasn't able to meet the retirement goals he had set for himself. His ultimate goal was compromised because he didn't have access to, or didn't act on, financial advice that might have helped him get what he wanted.

For someone who worked as long and as hard as he did, this setback was preventable.

CHOOSING YOUR FUTURE

Retirement is full of choices. To make good choices, you need information. Scratch that—you need **good** information. Retiring means you become responsible for providing your own paycheck for the rest of your life, and the decisions you make will continue to impact your financial health and lifestyle for ten, twenty, or thirty years.

Finding good, relevant information is critical. You won't find it just in conversations with a stockbroker. You won't find it by contacting an insurance salesperson, either. You won't even find it by merely calling the Social Security Administration.

They all have plenty of information, but it may not be information that will benefit you specifically. In some cases, this information may be designed more for mass consumption than for achieving **your** personal goals or meeting **your** individual needs in retirement. It may be too general in nature to be helpful, or it may sometimes be biased to meet the needs of their respective companies.

Having sat on both sides of the desk, I've come to appreciate how money represents more than the paper it's printed on. Money is the embodiment of your time, your talents, and your commitments. It buys the food you eat, the house you live in, the car you drive, the clothes you wear, and the care you provide for your loved ones. It also helps you realize the lifestyle you want to live in retirement.

Planning for retirement is really about planning for your future. After leaving behind the long hours, meetings, phone calls, office politics, stress, and everything else you won't miss about working, retirement planning is about replacing one thing you will miss: your paycheck.

Establishing a dependable stream of income that will last as long as you do is a key component to ensuring you will be able to enjoy retirement on your terms. To do this, I strongly believe you have to make decisions today that can positively affect your retirement and your quality of life in the years to come. We will explore options to do just that throughout this book.

To start, you have to survey the landscape, observe what's happening around you, and make decisions based on that information. The world is now a smaller place that moves faster, and changes seem to occur overnight whether we want them to or not. It's often hard to keep up with what's going on.

This is why consulting a professional who does keep up with the changing world, especially the financial one, is vital. To supplement, this book will cover many different concepts, ideas, and financial products, and it includes a glossary section at the end that serves as a quick reference guide for terms you may not fully understand. At the end of the day, this is a book of high-level information to get you thinking. I wouldn't ever recommend anything specific without knowing more about who you are and what you want for your future. Such knowledge comes only from a sustained relationship, one I am eager to establish with you.

All my best,

Tom Gandolfi,

Investment Adviser Representative,

Three Bridges Financial Group

CHAPTER ONE

Will I Have Enough Money in Retirement?

S everal years ago, my wife bought me a statuette for my office. The sculpture is of an elegant hand with its fingers crossed.

I keep it in my office to remind me that I don't want my clients to merely *hope* they'll have enough money for retirement. Instead, I want them to *know* whether they will have enough.

We spend our entire working lives hoping what we put into our retirement accounts will help us live comfortably once we clock out for the last time. Again, the key word in that sentiment, and the word that can make retirement feel like a looming problem instead of a rewarding life stage, is *hope*. We *hope* we will have money that lasts as long as we do.

Leaving your retirement to chance is unadvisable by nearly any standard, yet millions of people find themselves hoping instead of planning for what should be the best years of their lives. Creating a successful retirement plan with the right information, tools, and professional guidance puts you in better control of your financial future.

Let's talk for a moment about the difference between retirement saving and retirement planning.

Many people I meet during an initial visit to my office quickly disclose retirement assets they have amassed. I applaud them for their foresight and commitment.

They've likely made contributions to their company-sponsored 401(k) for years. They may have a personal individual retirement account (IRA) and/or a Roth IRA as well. They usually have some life insurance, or an insurance-backed annuity contract or two. They often own mutual funds, either stock- or bond-related, and they may also own some individual stocks in a brokerage account. They've recognized the need to invest in their future—for a time when they no longer have to work. Kudos to them for their diligence.

At the same time, many of these same insightful people have no idea how their retirement sources fit together as part of an overall retirement income plan.

Sure, they've done a nice job of saving and investing, but they haven't given enough thought to how and when to take retirement income from these assets. They haven't thought enough about when to begin drawing Social Security. What retirement assets should be tapped first for income, and which ones should be allowed to continue to grow? What plan provides long-term health care should it become necessary? What, if anything, will be left in the estate for any heirs?

Beyond those questions, many people I meet have their retirement assets scattered all over the financial globe. Their 401(k) is in one place, and their IRA is in another. They might have certificates of deposit (CDs) with different banks in different parts of the country. Maybe they purchased life insurance through an agent long-since retired, or they have annuities with different insurance companies. When inevitable questions about coverage or income options arise, they have no idea who to contact. Perhaps they want to leave something to their heirs but haven't done any legacy planning because, well, who likes talking about their own demise?

ORGANIZING YOUR ASSETS

Forgive me if I sound overly critical of people who haven't done extensive retirement planning—even the ones who have been working toward and talking about retirement with their financial professional for years still don't truly know what their financial picture looks like. That's why I'm here to help.

Often, I find it useful to compare people's investment and retirement portfolios to their homes.

Many people approaching retirement have lived in the same house for twenty or thirty years. The amount of stuff they've accumulated over that time can be mind-boggling. Just like antiques, old clothes, tools, books, and shoes, your financial products can also clutter your life. Eventually, this mountain of clutter may grow too vast for you to even think about dealing with it. It doesn't take long before you lose track of everything.

Yet, you can sort out the clutter by working with someone willing to wade through the mess and help you organize. One of the most important things I do with clients is help simplify their financial lives through consolidation and organization.

You are likely aware of most of your investments. You do read those monthly, quarterly, or annual statements, don't you? Yet you may not know the details about each one or how they work as part of an overall income plan. This is understandable. You are doing your best to prepare for retirement, and, though you have done a pretty good job, you probably will only retire once. How many of us do a perfect job the first time we do something all by ourselves?

This is why I emphasize the importance of working with someone who has prepared a financial or retirement plan more than once, twice, or even three times. In fact, you want to work with a professional who helps people retire every day, who works individually with their whole picture in mind and in their best interest. Because when you retire, you need to do more than a "pretty good job" of planning.

Building a retirement plan begins by defining the goals and needs you have for the future. This will highlight the purpose of your retirement plan and allow you to create strategies to help your assets achieve or even exceed these goals.

Having a personal conversation about these goals with your financial professional will give you the footing you need to move forward and make good decisions. The task ahead has many complexities, but it boils down to a core principle—structure your assets to create a dependable income for your life and achieve your financial goals.

Saving money for retirement and planning your retirement income are two different but equally important things. A detailed, quality retirement plan identifies why you own each asset and helps position your money to work as efficiently for you as possible.

You want strategies to leverage the money you have earned and saved over the years. To build and implement successful strategies, you first need to understand what assets you have, how they perform, why you have them, and what purpose they are designed to fulfill. In short, you need to be organized. Organizing your assets will help you see what steps you need to take to move forward, while helping you understand each asset's exposure to risk.

A retirement professional can provide tremendous assistance in this.

HOW MUCH RISK ARE YOU EXPOSED TO?

One key aspect of retirement planning is determining the chances your assets have of sustaining through an extended period of retirement.

Understanding how to manage your assets requires risk management, risk diversification, tax planning, and income planning preparation throughout your life stages. We'll talk about each of these areas throughout the book, but first, let's take a look at risk management.

If you are like many investors, you have no idea how much risk your money is truly exposed to. Organizing your assets can give you a better understanding of how much money is at risk.

To start, make a list that divides your assets into three kinds of money. Each of these can play a key role in insuring you have the kind of retirement you have worked for.

"Lifestyle money" is money you will use to build a stream of retirement income to last the rest of your life. This is the income you will want in order to pay your usual bills and continue living the life you're accustomed to. There are many different financial products that fall into this category, but they all will generally earn interest or dividends.

Examples of lifestyle money:
• Corporate bonds
• Preferred stocks
• Rental real estate
• Social Security
• Fixed indexed annuities
• Dividend stocks
• Real estate investment trusts (REITs)

Interest and dividends of these assets help establish a stream of income not solely dependent on stock market returns. Many people discover either their portfolios don't hold any of these types of investments, or, if they do, they don't have the ability to generate enough income to support their lifestyle. Later in the book we will address how to alleviate this.

"Growth money" is generally money you don't need right away in retirement. A majority of the people I meet have most of their money in these investments. Growth investments are usually offered in 401(k), 403(b), or other company-sponsored retirement plans. When you are working and contributing to your savings, your goal is to "grow" your money so you can one day retire. Once in retirement, most of us will still want a portion of our funds to address growth for future needs.

Examples of growth money:
• Growth stocks
• Stock mutual funds
• Index funds

"Comfort money" is exactly what it sounds like. It's money that makes you feel comfortable because it is easy to see and touch. It is also protected or insured. This is your security blanket. The low interest-rate environment makes it difficult to earn enough return with this money to keep pace with inflation, but it does feel good to have it!

Examples of comfort money:
• Savings accounts
• Checking accounts
• CDs
• Treasury bonds
• Money market accounts

Determining your appropriate level of risk is dependent on a number of variables. You need to feel comfortable with where and how you are investing your money, and your financial professional is obligated to help you make decisions to put your money in places within your risk criteria.

Your retirement plan must first meet your day-to-day income needs. How much money will you need to pay bills and other fixed expenses? How much money do you need to maintain your lifestyle? When do you need it? How, and from what sources, will you receive it? How much might you need for unforeseen, but not unexpected, health care concerns?

Managing your risk by having a balance of "lifestyle" vs. "growth" money is a good start. But how much "lifestyle" money is enough to secure your lifestyle needs during retirement? How much "growth" money is enough to allow you to continue to benefit from an improving market?

The average investor needs a retirement plan that provides income during retirement, potential for future growth, and legacy planning. This inevitably requires some degree of risk because "lifestyle" money, while more reliable and dependable, doesn't have the potential to grow as fast. "Growth" money, while more volatile, has more potential to increase in value over a period of time. "Growth" money can become "lifestyle" money later in retirement, if needed. Everyone's risk diversification will be different depending on their goals, age, and existing assets.

So, how do you decide how much risk your assets should be exposed to? Where do you begin? While the best course of action is to speak with a financial professional who can help you take a look at your comprehensive situation, there's also a handy guideline you can use to start making decisions about risk management.

THE RULE OF 100

The Rule of 100 is a general guideline to help shape asset diversification[1] for the average investor. The rule states that the percentage of an investor's assets exposed to risk is a number determined by the investor's age subtracted from 100.

• The Rule of 100: 100 - (your age) = the percentage of your assets exposed to risk (growth money)

• 100 - (30 years of age) = 70 percent

For example, if you are a thirty-year-old investor, the Rule of 100 suggests you should invest primarily in the market, engaging in a substantial amount of risk in your portfolio. It suggests that 70 percent of your investments should be in equities or market-risk investments while 30 percent should be in fixed income investments.

---

[1] *Diversification and asset allocation do not assure or guarantee better performance and cannot eliminate the risk of investment loss. Before investing, you should carefully read the applicable volatility disclosure for each of the underlying funds, which can be found in the current prospectus. Rule of 100 is a guideline; it is not intended to be used as the sole basis for financial decisions, nor should it be construed as advice designed to meet the particular needs of an individual's situation.*

Now, not every thirty-year-old should have exactly 70 percent of their assets in mutual funds and stocks. The Rule of 100 is based on your chronological age, not your "financial age," which could vary based on your investment experience, your aversion to or acceptance of risk, your planned retirement date, and other factors. While this guideline isn't an ironclad rule for anyone's finances, it's a good rule of thumb.

When you were age thirty and just starting your investment career, it made sense to have 70 percent of your money in the market. You had time on your side, meaning you had time to recover from a market downturn. You were still working, earning a predictable income and continuing, hopefully, to make investments as best you could.

Beyond that, you were most likely not taking income (i.e., you did not have to sell shares to generate revenue) from those investments at age thirty. Retirement was ages away, and your earning power was increasing. If the market took a corrective hit, you rode out the drought and waited for the next growing season. You believed the potential reward of long-term involvement in the market was worth a certain element of risk. Such is the province of youth.

Risk tolerance generally decreased as you aged, however. If you are forty years old and lose 30 percent of your portfolio in a market downturn, you might have twenty or thirty years to recover it. If you are sixty-eight years old, you likely won't have that kind of time to make a recovery.

That last circumstance changes your whole investment perspective. At age sixty-eight, it's likely you simply aren't as interested in suffering through a tough stock market. The time to recover from downturns is shorter, the stakes are higher, and the tolerance for risk is lower. The money you have saved is money you will soon need for income.

To start, you can use the Rule of 100. Then, make real changes once you've taken the time to look at your assets with a professional to determine your individual risk exposure, comfort level, and actual goals.

Personally, I'm a goals-based planner. When I work with a client, I first try to figure out what they want. For example, some people have income needs to support a specific lifestyle. They want to budget X amount for travel, X amount for their local church, and X amount a year in savings for their grandkids. Those are specific goals, and running an asset allocation model based on the Rule of 100 isn't necessarily going to meet those goals.

THE ROLE OF COMPOUND EARNINGS

When discussing the role of growth in your portfolio, it's important to not overlook compound earnings.

Compounded earnings can have incredible power over time. The longer your money has time to compound, the greater your wealth will be. This is what most people talk about when they refer to putting their money to work. This is also why the young can afford a higher tolerance of risk.

If you start investing when you are young, you can invest smaller amounts of money in a more aggressive fashion because you have the potential to 1) make a profit in a rising market, and 2) harness the power of compounded earnings. But when you are forty, fifty, or sixty years old, that long-term growth potential shrinks alongside your risk tolerance. You are forced to keep more money invested in lower-risk vehicles in order to receive anything close to the return you might have known as a younger person. Basically, it becomes more expensive to wisely invest the older you get.

When it comes to risk tolerance, even a good rule of thumb will fall short because your age is only one factor. The size of your portfolio, your lifestyle, personal comfort, goals, retirement date, health, and a myriad of other decisions will all play a role in your investment decisions.

A financial professional can look at your assets and discuss alternatives to optimize your balance between promise and potential money.

CHAPTER TWO

The Color of Money

L et's put some additional perspective on why we spend the time we do talking about risk management in retirement planning.

The reason seems obvious, but it is a point that bears repeating: *When you are in retirement and no longer receiving the regular paycheck you counted on during your years in the work force, you must now use your own assets to build your personal ATM—a money machine with income when you need it for as long as you need it. This income is generated from the retirement assets you've amassed through all those years of saving and investing.*

An equally important second point:

To be sure your income machine continues to function for as long as you do—for as long as you live—it is essential to know how much risk your investments face. Sadly, far too many retirement investors don't realize the level of risk to which the assets they will depend on for life are exposed.

Risk is a part of investing, to be sure. The expression "no risk, no reward," has been driven into our investing brains almost as much as "buy low, sell high." While there is still room for some risk in retirement planning, there is also a need to seek protection against losing money you simply can't afford to lose.

In a nutshell, one of the best approaches I've seen involves making a thorough inventory of all retirement assets and assigning a color to each. Each color represents a level of risk. The colors help investors better visualize their risk and truly adjust for their comfort level.

In this case, we'll use the colors red, yellow, and green to designate risk level. These are the colors of a typical traffic signal, and they have some of the same meanings in this approach.

STOP AND LOOK AT YOUR RED MONEY

Let's start with what we call "red money."

Red doesn't mean coming to a complete stop in this analogy, but the color is meant to catch your attention. Red represents the assets you want to grow aggressively. Growth of your assets is a wonderful goal we all share, but there is a significant downside when investing only for growth. That downside potential deserves your attention, hence the color red.

Red money refers to investments at risk through exposure to the natural ups and downs of the stock market or other economic forces. It has the potential to grow, but it can also decline in value. The trouble, of course, is that you have no idea—neither do I—of which direction the market will turn at any specific time.

Sure, market history in our country has shown us strong growth over a long period of time, but such growth is not consistent. At periods of time the market does very well, while at others performance is dismal. The challenge of planning for retirement is considering how you will determine when and which way the market will turn.

The short answer is, you won't, and neither will I or any other financial planner or broker. Yes, we can all watch for economic indicators, evaluate the state of the economy, and guess based on the available information, but the market can change quickly. In fact, it changes faster now than just twenty or thirty years ago.

A rise in market value generally produces the return on red money, called capital appreciation (an increase in share value). Capital appreciation in a growth-based investment is the primary source of growth. This makes appreciating assets different from financial products that generate most of their return by earning interest and/or dividends. Some red money investments are also capable of generating dividends, but the main reason for choosing red investments is for capital appreciation.

Red money should be considered growth money—money you may need someday, but not necessarily today or tomorrow. This is money you may want for future health care, a grandchild's college education, or for your loved ones. It could—and perhaps should, in my opinion—be money you might want to spend on your own personal retirement ambitions, such as that dream vacation or vacation home.

You don't, however, want to rely exclusively on red money for essential income, especially during market downturns. Taking income by selling equity shares during such times is a direct violation of the "buy low, sell high" advice you've heard forever. In retirement, you want to put yourself in position to sell red money assets when you *want*, not because you *have* to do so. We'll discuss ways to help do this elsewhere in this chapter.

Examples of red money include:
• Stocks
• Mutual funds (all of them, including bond funds)
• Exchange-traded funds (ETFs)
• Variable annuities
• Commodities, such as gold and silver.

Again, these are at-risk investments whose value will ebb and flow with the daily fluctuations of the stock market.

GREEN MONEY: IT'S GOOD TO GO

Green money is not only limited to cash, but it also involves assets offering protection against loss of principal due to market fluctuations. Green money is part of the "comfortable" money we discussed in Chapter 1. It is reasonably liquid, meaning it should be relatively easy to access when you need cash for immediate needs.

I call green money "defensive money" as a way of distinguishing it from red money on the offense side of the ball. Green money has some potential for growth, but the low-interest climate after the Great Recession limits those prospects. It is not considered a growth asset, though it is as an essential part of a retirement portfolio.

Examples of green money assets and the principal protection they provide include:

BANK/MONEY MARKET ACCOUNTS

These accounts, some of the safest forms of investments available, began making a comeback around 2018. Bank certificates of deposit (CDs) largely fell out of favor in the years following the Great Recession. To promote borrowing and spending in order to jump-start the sluggish economy of the time, the Federal Reserve cut interest rates to almost nothing. It became cheap and easy to borrow money, but it also meant banks paid safety-conscious savers—once the unheralded heroes of American investing—next to nothing on their savings and CD deposits.

With Fed decisions in 2017 and 2018 to increase interest rates in a more robust economy, CDs started regaining interest, literally and figuratively. With more CDs offering interest rates of 1 to 2 percent higher, safety-conscious savers began turning back to an old friend with FDIC protection against losses of up to $250,000. The concept of "laddering" CDs—amassing certificates of different durations—seems to be an option again in these higher-interest times.

U.S. TREASURY BONDS

Investors seeking the generation of interest income along with some kind of safety net often turn to Uncle Sam and the U.S. Treasury bonds he offers. As in the case of CDs, Treasury bonds usually aren't very exciting, but they offer interest income and are backed by the full faith and credit of the U.S. government.

In August 2019, the ten-year Treasury note, a benchmark note for comparison purposes, was yielding about 1.6 percent. Again, not too thrilling, but it does pay about 1.6 percent in annual interest with very little risk. Treasury bonds, like CDs, are available in varying time frames ranging from a few months to thirty years. Note that, like CDs, the longer the maturity date, the higher the bond's rate of interest.

SOCIAL SECURITY

Social Security is included here among green-money assets because it represents the return on an investment you made, however involuntarily, through mandatory payroll deductions during your working days. We'll discuss the long-term viability of Social Security in more detail in Chapter 5, but for now let me simply say I believe Social Security will continue to be a source of sustained income throughout the lifetimes of most readers of this book.

YELLOW MONEY: AN IMPORTANT COMBINATION OF RED AND GREEN

Just as a yellow traffic signal represents a transition from green to red, yellow money is a hybrid of green and red money. More significantly, it represents what I view as an essential component of any successful retirement portfolio.

Yellow money assets are those in which the majority of growth comes primarily through the generation of interest and dividends. This is income generation *not solely* dependent on market performance. As is the case with red money, these products have the potential for growth, though income is prioritized more than growth. The growth potential for most assets is unknown, but the projected interest or dividends to be generated are more clearly defined. Not all yellow money assets have protection against loss of principal, but they are less volatile and not highly dependent on fluctuations of the stock market.

In my opinion, this combination of income-producing capability (regardless of market performance) and potential for growth, makes yellow money the foundation upon which a retirement income plan is based. Let me explain.

As I discussed in the introduction to this book, I believe a foundation of "yellow money"—assets that produce sustained income while avoiding significant volatility—is essential in order to make good judgments affecting the growth of red money.

Examples of yellow money assets, and reasoning for their placement in this category, include:

CORPORATE AND MUNICIPAL BONDS

The interest rate paid on these bonds is defined by the "coupon rate." The bond's "maturity date" sets the future point in time at which the "par value" of the bond—the principal you paid to purchase the bond—is returned to the investor. (Note: Bonds can rise or fall in value if traded before the maturity date.) The ability to pay interest and return the par value of the bond at maturity is backed by the financial stability of the corporation or municipality issuing the bond.

Municipal bonds made lots of money for people in the past and were once a favorite vehicle for retirement. They are a bit more challenging today because the yields are relatively low. A municipal bond today might produce interest between 2 and 3 percent, sometimes as high as 3.5 percent.

When you buy municipal bonds, as with any bond, you are purchasing that entity's debt on their promise to pay interest as well as return your invested principal at maturity. So, your investment is backed by the credit of the municipality issuing them. With some municipalities facing financial distress and lower credit ratings than they once enjoyed, some "muny" bonds today aren't always as safe as they once were. They do offer potential tax advantages, but the yields are pretty low. Consequently, many "muny" bonds aren't as attractive as they used to be, but there is a safety net supporting them—the ability of the issuing municipality to pay its debts to bondholders.

Corporate bonds are different from the mutual bond funds familiar to many people. These are individual bonds issued by corporations. When you purchase such a bond, you receive two key guarantees. The first is a maturity date, which is the point in the future when you can expect to receive all of your invested principal. The second guarantee is a coupon rate dictating the amount of annual interest you will acquire for as long as you hold the bond.

Corporate bonds also come in different types, with the most conservative called "investment grade." These bonds are issued by the most financially sound companies with the best credit ratings. Your principal invested with these companies is relatively safe, though not guaranteed. Investment grade bonds today typically yield somewhere between 3.5 and 4.5 percent.

Another type is higher-yield corporate bonds. These are not necessarily the same as "junk bonds," but not everyone knows the difference. They are issued by companies whose financial stability may be slightly lower than companies offering investment grade bonds. They often yield somewhere between 4.5 and 6.5 percent in today's environment.

I will skip a discussion of junk bonds here because, frankly, I don't believe in them or find them appropriate for someone in retirement. Their potential for greater yield comes from their volatility and elevated risk.

FIXED INDEX ANNUITIES

These insurance contracts have potential to grow in value through credited interest generated by any rise in the market index designated in the contract. The contract holder's participation rate in the rise of the index is determined by terms of the contract. The annuity contract also guarantees against loss of principal due to market volatility. When the contract holder is ready to begin taking income from the annuity, the contractual guarantee is backed by the claims-paying ability of the insurance company issuing the contract. (Look for a more detailed discussion on annuities in Chapter 6, "Filling the Income Gap.")

PREFERRED STOCK

Preferred stocks are different than common stock. For one thing, they generate a higher rate of return, much more like a bond than a stock. Preferred stocks are exactly what the name suggests: the shareholders who own them are preferred, meaning they are the first to receive dividends, and they receive the highest dividends. Preferred stocks generally have a par value, and the returns are typically generated by the dividends they pay. In today's climate, a preferred stock might pay dividends of anywhere from 5 to 7.5 percent.

REAL ESTATE AND/OR REAL ESTATE INVESTMENT TRUSTS (REITS)

Owning real estate has long been a source of income for people in or near retirement. Real estate can produce rental income along with potential for growth if a property is sold at a profit.

Investors also have the opportunity to participate in the income-producing potential of real estate without actually owning property.

Participation in a real estate investment trust (REIT) gives an investor a share in a company that manages real estate and conducts real estate transactions. As that company collects, rents, or makes profits from the sale of property, a portion of that income is returned to the REIT's shareholders as a dividend.

REITs, however, can be volatile and very sensitive to interest rate changes, as are other real estate transactions. They are not always appropriate for people in retirement, but those who feel comfortable with the risk have seen returns of between 6 and 9 percent during the writing of this book in 2019.

BUSINESS DEVELOPMENTS COMPANIES (BDCS)

BDCs are financial institutions focused primarily on business-to-business opportunities. Their primary market involves investing in, or making development capital available to, small to mid-size companies—mostly start-up ventures. They differ from venture capital funds where participation is typically limited to large financial institutions and wealthy investors. Participation in a BDC, on the other hand, is available even to smaller investors.

Income for such investors is created through dividends generated by the companies in which the BDC invests. A BDC, in short, allows an investor to participate in the growth of small and medium-size business without actually owning stock in those companies. BDC shares can trade like stock, meaning they have some market volatility. In today's environment, a BDC might pay dividends of about 5.5 to 8.5 percent.

LIMITED PARTNERSHIPS (LPS)

A limited partner in a business arrangement shares in the profits and losses of the business, but the liability for losses or debts is limited to the amount of capital originally invested. A general partner typically runs the business and is wholly responsible for losses or debts. As with many other kinds of investments, investors have the potential to earn dividends based on the generated profits generated.

WHY I LIKE YELLOW-MONEY ASSETS

Bonds are a prime example of why I like yellow-money assets. This is because the vast return from a bond derives from the interest the bond pays. Bonds aren't expected to double in value—they are intended to be an income-producing asset, not a growth asset. However, the bond has a maturity date (the point when the bonded entity agrees to pay out the full par value of the bond). It's our safety mechanism. During the time we hold the bond, we receive a known rate of interest as determined by the bond's coupon rate. I especially prefer this kind of income-producing investment for people in retirement.

Let's say in 2018 you invest $100,000 in a portfolio of ten-year corporate bonds that have a par value of $100,000. The bonds have a maturity date in September 2028. The bonds all have a coupon of 4.5 percent. You plan to hold the bonds for the full ten years.

Over that time, the value of the bonds will fluctuate as the bond market ebbs and flows, but that's not your primary concern if you don't intend to trade the bonds. Your intent is to hold the portfolio to maturity, at which time you get back the par value of the bonds: your entire $100,000 principal. During the ten years you hold the bond, it pays the 4.5 percent coupon rate on an annual basis, a predictable stream of income.

What income might such a bond produce?

On a $100,000 corporate bond with a ten-year maturity and a 4.5 percent coupon rate, you will be paid $4,500 a year each year over the ten years you hold the bond, or $45,000 in total. At the end of ten years, you also get back your $100,000 initial payment.

While the value of the bond might vary if traded before maturity—it could be worth more or less than $100,000—the bond is still paying $4,500 a year regardless of whether the bond market goes up or down. Again, such income production is what I like about yellow money.

Let's now look at real estate, which can be composed of either red or yellow money.

Let's say you just received a $250,000 inheritance, and you want to invest the money rather than spend it on a fancy new car and a kitchen remodel. (Good for you!—not everyone is this frugal.)

You decide to make a real estate investment, and you have multiple choices. You might buy a piece of undeveloped land to sit on in the hope that, over time, it will gain in value until you decide to either develop it or sell it.

This is a red money investment, like a market-risk stock.

Your other real estate option with that $250,000 is to buy property with a tenant who has, say, a ten-year lease. He's signed up to pay you $12,000 in rent annually for the next ten years. This property may or may not appreciate over time, but the payments you receive for rent will continue for all ten years whether the value goes up or not. This is yellow money, as your investment is producing known and predictable income.

Which deal do you want—the bird in hand or the one in the bush? It's an individual decision, entirely up to you, but I personally like the idea of *knowing* I have established income rather than *hoping* I might achieve future growth.

GROWTH IS GOOD, BUT NEVER GUARANTEED

Please don't misunderstand me here. I have nothing against red money. I love growth, and I wish all accounts would experience it.

But the market experiences daily ups and downs, gains and losses. These are inevitable. Having a portion of your retirement assets in yellow, income-producing assets gives you at least some degree of support. These are assets you know will produce income regardless of whether the market goes up or down. This foundation reduces the pressure to sell red money assets during down-market cycles to generate essential income. Such selling decisions can adversely affect the long-term health of your retirement savings.

The next chapter discusses sequence risk—the concept of how decisions made early in your retirement can have a dramatic and occasionally undesirable effect on your retirement savings. We'll talk in more detail about how a foundation of yellow money might help you avoid having to sell red-money resources at the worst possible times.

Until then, let me restate my opinion. So much of a successful retirement plan depends on how we structure the assets we've amassed during our working years.

People invest money looking for a total return. Some return will come from growth, some from income. The way most people invest—mainly because Wall Street tells them to—is by putting money into mutual funds, where the vast majority of return is generated through market growth. This generates minimal income or dividends.

I have a different viewpoint. I believe it's much more appropriate and often more effective for people in retirement to derive a higher percentage of their total return from things we can count on—specifically, interest and dividends. While these are not completely guaranteed, they are more predictable than market-based growth or capital appreciation. We never know how much the stock market will rise or fall from week to week or year to year. But, if we have investments with a defined interest rate or a defined dividend, we at least have some measure of predictability regarding the return.

TO EVERYTHING THERE IS A REASON

I believe each investment in a person's portfolio should have a specific goal. You probably shouldn't invest in a random collection of stocks, mutual funds, and bonds, hoping at least some of them flourish. Unfortunately, this seems to be a common approach.

Red money investments have growth potential and are exposed to market risk. That should be your expectation. When investing in these assets, you are making a risk-vs-reward calculation, hoping for a favorable result but accepting that results are unpredictable when your money is exposed to market risk.

Green money investments are comfortable to own. They have a goal of safety with some liquidity. They should offer some form of principal protection as part of the investment. This does not mean all green money investments are 100 percent protected, though, as any investment can experience some kind of loss. (Even bank CDs might experience an element of loss if interest doesn't keep up with the rate of inflation.) Still, the purpose of green money is to provide some kind of safety net for at least a portion of your portfolio.

The purpose of yellow money assets is to create sustainable income by paying dividends and interest. This income can help support everyday living expenses, taxes, a lifestyle dream, or legacy giving.

Equally important, having predictable income helps reduce some of the panic decisions people make when they have to sell market-exposed red money assets to generate necessary income during a market downturn. Having predictable income elsewhere allows red money investments to sit and wait out market downturns.

Yellow money can be one of your primary tools to achieve your retirement goals. Not only does it generate income through predictable interest and dividends, but its exposure to less market risk also reduces the level of volatility in a retirement portfolio.

What I try to do with a retirement portfolio is encourage people into a tighter range of risk tolerance. How tight depends on the individual's risk tolerance and personal goals but taking on less risk in retirement generally leads to a higher likelihood for retirement savings to outlive the investor.

I often see clients arrive with a portfolio of nothing but mutual funds. I'm glad to see them investing, but usually this kind of portfolio has a 20 to 50 percent downside risk with only 20 to 30 percent upside potential. That's a wide variation of potential outcomes. You'll have to decide if this is your best path forward.

I prefer to tighten the range to somewhere between down 5 percent and up 15 percent, or down 10 and up 20. A tighter range of possible outcomes increases the likelihood of success.

PORTFOLIO DIVERSIFICATION

One final note on retirement portfolio management.

When building a sound portfolio, especially for retirees, investment diversification is vital. You do not want to put everything into one company's stock or one corporation's bonds, and you also want diversification among the different types of money.

It makes sense for most people to have some red, some yellow, and some green money. How much goes where is specific to each individual and their goals but having diversity among several baskets is as essential as having diversity within each basket.

CHAPTER THREE

Managing Risk Factors

Being able to visualize and subsequently organize your retirement assets into risk categories such as red, yellow, and green money is integral to avoiding risk. But there are other equally important risk factors to address when evaluating the long-term viability of your retirement portfolio.

Outside of market risk, other risk factors include fluctuating interest rates, required minimum distributions from your tax-deferred accounts, and taxes.

Another crucial yet overlooked risk factor interplaying with market risk is called sequence risk.

For many people, sequence risk is something they have little control over, yet it can have a considerable effect on their retirement investments. Sequence risk may even present the largest potential threat to a retiree's financial security.

Surprisingly, though, you aren't likely to read much about it in investment publications or hear it discussed on cable TV financial channels. Most stockbrokers and financial salespeople don't talk much about it, preferring instead to focus on future potential and encouraging strategies more appropriate for younger investors. Despite the lack of coverage, sequence risk in the early years of retirement is a lurking danger that can dramatically impact your retirement plan.

Sequence risk, also called "sequence of return risk," is simply the risk of receiving low or negative returns early in your retirement or in the years leading up to your retirement. Put another way, people early in retirement who take income from red money market-risk investments during market downturns increase the potential of falling into a financial hole, causing damage to the long-term viability of their retirement plan.

I consider the five years before and five years after retirement to be the "hot zone" for sequence risk.

If your plan is to use "traditional" growth investment strategies into retirement, you must hope for a good sequence of returns in the hot zone. If you don't, it could have a lasting negative impact on your financial reality in retirement.

Let's look at a hypothetical example showing the impact that sequence risk might have on a retirement income plan and your life savings.

MIKE AND MICHELLE: SIMILAR BEGINNINGS, DRAMATICALLY DIFFERENT ENDINGS

Siblings Mike and Michelle, separated in age by four years, were both successful in their careers.

Through hard work, they each saved $1 million by the time they retired at age sixty-two. They both decided to continue investing their retirement portfolios in a fund closely following the S&P 500 index. This index fund served them well while they were working and contributing to their retirement accounts. They believed they could depend on their savings to grow over time, even though they would likely be selling some of their shares and withdrawing a portion of their savings each year to support their lifestyles in retirement.

Big brother Mike retired in 1996 at age sixty-two. From 1996 to 2000 he enjoyed impressive returns from the market. He withdrew 4 percent of his original portfolio value each year for income, adjusted annually for inflation, just like his broker advised.

Using this method, after four years of taking 4 percent withdrawals, Mike's account had more than doubled in value. His $1 million had grown to over $2 million during a period in which the S&P 500 experienced annual growth of 20, 31, 26.6 and 19.5 percent. Mike believed he had reached the financial security he had worked hard to achieve.

Mike was the benefactor of a positive sequence of returns in the first four years of his retirement. Twenty years later, at the age of eighty-two, he still had $1.64 million in his retirement account (based on the historical returns of the S&P 500 through 2016). There is very little chance his lifestyle will suffer in his later years.

Mike Matthew's Retirement Income Plan					
Investment Amount: $1,000,000 Investment Strategy: S&P 500 ETF Beginning Month/Year: 1996 Ending Month/Year: 2016			Annual Income Withdrawal: 4% Annual Income Withdrawal Cost of Living Adjustment: 3%		
Year	Beginning Value	One-Year Index Return	Change in Value Income	Annual Withdrawal	Year-End Value
1996	$1,000,000	20.26%	$202,600	$40,000	$1,162,600
1997	$1,162,600	31.01%	$360,522	$41,200	$1,481,922
1998	$1,481,922	26.67%	$395,229	$42,436	$1,834,715
1999	$1,834,715	19.53%	$358,320	$43,709	$2,149,326
2000	$2,149,326	-10.14%	-$217,942	$45,020	$1,886,364
2001	$1,886,364	-13.04%	-$245,982	$46,371	$1,594,011
2002	$1,594,011	-23.37%	-$372,520	$47,762	$1,173,728
2003	$1,173,728	26.38%	$309,630	$49,195	$1,434,163
2004	$1,434,163	8.99%	$128,931	$50,671	$1,512,424
2005	$1,512,424	3.00%	$45,373	$52,191	$1,505,605
2006	$1,505,605	13.62%	$205,063	$53,757	$1,656,912
2007	$1,656,912	3.52%	$58,323	$55,369	$1,659,866
2008	$1,659,866	-38.49%	-$638,882	$57,030	$963,953
2009	$963,953	23.45%	$226,047	$58,741	$1,131,259
2010	$1,131,259	12.78%	$144,575	$60,504	$1,215,330
2011	$1,215,330	0.00%	$0	$62,319	$1,153,011
2012	$1,153,011	13.41%	$154,619	$64,188	$1,243,442
2013	$1,243,442	29.60%	$368,059	$66,114	$1,545,387
2014	$1,545,387	11.39%	$176,020	$68,097	$1,653,309
2015	$1,653,309	-0.73%	-$12,069	$70,140	$1,571,100
2016	$1,571,100	9.54%	$149,883	$72,244	$1,648,738
Average One-Year Index Return: 8.37% Total Annual Withdrawal: $1,147,059 Total Change in Account Value: 64.87%					

These are hypothetical examples for illustrative purposes only. The hypothetical returns are not indicative of actual market performance. Actual market returns will vary. This is not intended to project the performance of any specific investment or index. It is not possible to invest directly in an index. If this were an actual product, the returns may be reduced by certain fees and expenses. Withdrawals are subject to ordinary income tax and, if taken prior to fifty-nine-and-a-half, a 10 percent federal tax penalty.

Michelle Matthew's Retirement Income Plan

Investment Amount: $1,000,000	Annual Income Withdrawal: 4%
Investment Strategy: S&P 500 ETF	Annual Income Withdrawal
Beginning Month/Year: 2000	Cost of Living Adjustment:
Ending Month/Year: 2016	3%

Year	Beginning Value	One-Year Index Return	Change in Value Income	Annual Withdrawal	Year-End Value
2000	$1,000,000	-10.14%	-$101,400	$40,000	$858,600
2001	$858,600	-13.04%	-$111,961	$41,200	$705,439
2002	$705,439	-23.37%	-$164,861	$42,436	$498,142
2003	$498,142	26.38%	$131,410	$43,709	$585,842
2004	$585,842	8.99%	$52,667	$45,020	$593,489
2005	$593,489	3.00%	$17,805	$46,371	$564,923
2006	$564,923	13.62%	$76,942	$47,762	$594,103
2007	$594,103	3.52%	$20,912	$49,195	$565,821
2008	$565,821	-38.49%	-$217,784	$50,671	$297,365
2009	$297,365	23.45%	$69,732	$52,191	$314,907
2010	$314,907	12.78%	$40,245	$53,757	$301,395
2011	$301,395	0.00%	$0	$55,369	$246,026
2012	$246,026	13.41%	$32,992	$57,030	$221,987
2013	$221,987	29.60%	$65,708	$58,741	$228,954
2014	$228,954	11.39%	$26,078	$60,504	$194,529
2015	$194,529	-0.73%	-$1,420	$62,319	$130,790
2016	$130,790	9.54%	$12,477	$64,188	$79,079

Average One-Year Index Return: 4.37%
Total Annual Withdrawal: $870,464
Total Change in Account Value: -92.09%

Please note, it is not possible to invest directly into the S&P 500® Index; this measure is provided solely as a gauge of overall market performance. Standard & Poor's: "Standard & Poor's®," "S&P®," and "S&P 500®" are registered trademarks of Standard & Poor's Financial Services LLC ("S&P"). The historical performance of the S&P 500 is not intended as an indication of its future performance and is not guaranteed. This chart is not intended to provide investment, tax, or legal advice. Be sure to consult a qualified professional about your individual situation. This chart does not take into account investment fees, so actual results may be different than depicted above.

Younger sister Michelle retired four years later in 2000, also at the age of sixty-two. Like her big brother, Michelle had accumulated $1 million in her retirement accounts and was invested in the same strategy as Mike. She also planned to withdraw 4 percent of her original portfolio value, adjusting for inflation, covering her income needs each year.

During her first year of retirement in the year 2000, the S&P 500 index was down slightly more than 10 percent in the first full year of the dot-com bubble burst. Michelle was a bit concerned, but she had experienced downturns before and was confident her portfolio would recover, just as it always had in the past.

What Michelle didn't take into account, however, was that she was no longer earning a paycheck and making contributions to her investments. She was instead depending on her savings to support her lifestyle, which required her to withdraw a portion of those savings. In order to take income, she had to sell shares in her retirement account and turn them into cash. Remember, Michelle and Mike are using the same strategy—their only difference is their retirement dates.

Unfortunately, over the next two years the market continued to decline—by 13 percent in 2001 and another 23 percent in 2002—and so did the balance in her retirement account. Just three years into retirement, over half of her initial $1 million account balance disappeared.

Even so, Michelle decided to stick with her strategy; her broker told her to "hang in there," and she knew the market historically always revives. Over the next five years, it did, and she was able to recover some of her losses while supporting her income needs.

Then appeared 2008 and a drop of almost 38.5 percent in the S&P 500. The toll on Michelle's retirement savings was devastating. Only sixteen years into retirement, Michelle is seventy-seven years old with less than $80,000 left in her account. Maintaining her current income, she is on schedule to run out of money in less than two years.

The difference between the projected performance of Mike's portfolio versus his sister's is both drastic and explainable.

For Mike, the story was written in the first four years he started taking income. His account grew so much in value during a period of strong market performance, he couldn't screw it up, even though there was the dot-com bubble burst and Great Recession just ahead.

Michelle, however, was beaten down from the start of her retirement by declining market conditions over which she had no control. One might second-guess her decision to hold onto devalued red money assets she needed for immediate income, but we shouldn't be overly harsh. After all, her belief the market would come back proved correct in the years from 2002 through 2007, and again after the Great Recession of 2008. Trouble is, when the market made its rise after the roller coaster drops of 2000 to '02 and '08, Michelle now had fewer shares to grow in value. She was in a hole that likely would take more time to escape than she had available.

THE OPPOSITE OF DOLLAR-COST AVERAGING

What Michelle experienced is part of the problem with basing too much of your retirement income strategy on the historical performance of the market. Sure, one can look at the 100-year historical performance of the S&P 500 and note it has risen an average of 8 percent over that time.

But ask yourself this: How many 100-year-old investors do you know? Remember too, the age-old financial services warning that past performance is no indication of future results. The history of the market may give us hope for a long-term future, but you already know what I think about pinning your retirement dreams on hope alone. The only market years concerning you upon nearing or entering retirement are the ones immediately ahead, not those of the past.

This is because things are different in retirement than they were in your working days. During those years you drew a regular paycheck and likely made regular investment contributions. In retirement, however, you are probably now taking income from those investments. The sequence of returns was irrelevant when you were adding instead of subtracting from your accounts, but once you start taking money out in retirement for whatever reason—because you need the income, you need to satisfy RMDs, or you want to take a dream vacation or buy a new car—the order of the returns becomes very important.

You are essentially engaging in reverse dollar-cost averaging.

Dollar-cost averaging is a concept we learn early in our investment life. We benefit from dollar-cost averaging when we make regular contributions to our IRAs or 401(k). When we make regular contributions while the market is depressed and prices are low, we are buying more shares with the same contribution. We average out somewhat when the market trends upward and the same contribution buys fewer shares when prices are higher.

When you are retired and start drawing money out of an investment account, the exact opposite happens. If you sell (to generate needed income) when the market is high, you sell fewer shares to produce the income you want. That's a good thing. But when the market is down, you must sell more shares at a lower price to generate the same level of income you want. Over time, you are dollar-cost averaging in reverse.

We've all been given the same investment advice since the day we saved our first dollar—buy low, sell high. When you take distributions while the market is low because of declines or corrections, you are doing the exact opposite. You are selling low.

TAKE SOME RISK OUT OF SEQUENCE RETURNS

The story of Mike and Michelle—hypothetical but based on the very real performance of the S&P 500—is shows the incredible power of sequence risk. You cannot control it since you have no idea where the market will turn tomorrow, this year, or in years ahead. And it can't be easily fixed once it happens.

Thus, before it happens, consider some things to mitigate sequence risk.

Taking some risk off the table can make the difference between a successful retirement and having to start a part-time job to pay the bills.

My alternative to taking distributions from red (at risk) money accounts during times when market prices are depressed is to employ a foundation of yellow money through periods of market declines.

Yellow money is generating income whether the market is shifting up or down. You're not forced to sell shares to generate income; instead, you have the opportunity to take income from interest and dividends generated by your yellow-money assets while your red money awaits a market rebound. This approach can make a substantial difference in the long-term performance of your retirement savings.

If you don't have adequate money in the yellow bucket—if the majority of your assets are red money—you will *have* to sell shares to generate income when necessary. But when you have money in the yellow bucket, those investments are generating income, allowing you the option to not sell red-money shares.

To help mitigate sequence risk, you might "carve out," or reallocate, a portion of your savings to income-producing assets safe from market risk. If you create a steady income stream with a portion of your assets using this strategy, you won't need to expose your entire portfolio, and the security of your retirement, to sequence risk. You can also retain some potential for growth with other market-risk assets.

UNDERSTANDING YOUR 401(K)

If you are like most Americans, you have contributed to one or more 401(k) plans (or their nonprofit or public employment equivalent), usually sponsored by your employer, during your working career.

Most plans let you choose from a limited set of investment options with little or no guidance from a professional. Most plans don't, however, let you know how the money is managed, what kind of fees you are paying, or to what level of risk your money is exposed.

Some 401(k)s include "target-date funds," designed to be weighted and rebalanced to account for people who are approaching retirement. Those options, however, didn't save millions of Americans from losing up to 30 percent of the value of their 401(k) plans during the 2008 market drop.

One of the major problems with 401(k) plans is the money in them is easily forgotten; out of sight, out of mind. Your contributions, automatically deducted from your paycheck, transfer into a tax-deferred account you attempt to keep your hands off of until you retire. The money is not in a bank or a protected account, however, and the companies administering 401(k) investments don't have active management duties. They present investors with a few investment choices, but otherwise you are on your own.

For many people, the money in their 401(k) represents a significant majority of their retirement savings. Wouldn't it make sense to take a more active role in ensuring such money is not exposed to more risk than necessary—especially as you approach retirement? If you haven't examined the performance of your 401(k) investment options since you picked them one, five, or ten years ago, it's time to reevaluate.

I'm not asking everyone to be a financial expert or to successfully predict the future. But I think it makes sense to know what you are invested in, why you are invested in it, and what goal you want your investments to achieve. Your 401(k), which likely is the largest retirement investment you have, should be at the top of your list for evaluation and analysis.

If you are uncomfortable with the way your 401(k) is organized, you have options. Have a conversation with the administrators of your plan to better understand what options apply to you. As you age, it is your responsibility to reposition your assets for safety and longevity.

FINDING THE RIGHT RISK BALANCE

Have you ever owned a Swiss Army Knife? If not, you are probably at least familiar with the handy pocket utility tool.

A Swiss Army Knife includes all kinds of interesting options. It contains a knife blade (often two), scissors, a file, a corkscrew, and even a screwdriver or two (flat head and Phillips head). It's a convenient novelty offering some utility value.

The trouble is, its value is limited, mainly because its various components aren't recognized for excellent performance.

They work, sure, but not especially well. The scissors don't cut well, the knife is usually dull, the file is too narrow, the screwdrivers are tiny, and the corkscrew is a true challenge. Just try to pull a cork from a bottle of wine with it. Yes, there is incredible potential in one pocket-carried device featuring a variety of tools, but it's a struggle to finish the task.

The image of a Swiss Army Knife illustrates how a retirement portfolio without the proper balance of risk and return might struggle to accomplish your goals.

One perceived benefit of the 401(k) is that many retirement investment options are all packaged together in one place. Yet, when you hold all your money in an investment account like a 401(k), any combination of stock mutual funds or other investment not well diversified from a risk perspective is like asking your money to be a Swiss Army Knife. You are asking it to do a lot of different jobs—grow, generate income, stay secure, etc. But, just like the knife, if you ask it to do everything, it won't do anything well.

Instead, you must evaluate what tools you are using and whether they are the best tools to achieve your goal.

CONSIDERING LONG-TERM CARE

With all the unknowns, figuring out exactly where you stand for retirement is tricky. Chief among the unknowns is long-term care. Most people don't know if they will need long-term care in the future, much less to what degree and for how long.

The one thing we do know is long-term care is expensive and will likely increase in price.

While most people realize long-term care is a possible future necessity, many fail to recognize its potential impact on their life savings and lifestyle in retirement.

According to the 2018 "Cost of Care Survey" prepared by Genworth Financial (an insurance company whose products include long-term care insurance), the average nationwide monthly charge for a semi-private room in a nursing care facility was $7,741. What? You don't like the idea of sharing a room? Genworth's survey found the nationwide average monthly cost of a private room in a nursing care facility to be $8,365. You might save some money if you can survive on adult day care (an estimated $1,560 per month), or even with home health care ($4,004 per month, according to the Genworth survey).[2] But then, who among us knows what level of long-term care we might need in the future?

We do know a few things, however. 1) Long-term care is becoming more probable as life expectancies lengthen, and 2) the cost of care isn't likely to decrease over time. In fact, prices for nursing home care increased an average of 2.4 percent annually from 2012 to 2019, for a cumulative increase of 20.7 percent. According to National Health Expenditure projections, home health care spending will increase 83 percent from 2018 to 2027. Expenditures for nursing homes and other retirement communities are projected to increase 58 percent during that period.[3]

---

[2] Genworth Financial Inc. June 2018. "Cost of care survey 2018."
https://www.genworth.com/aging-and-you/finances/cost-of-care.html
[3] American Action Forum. Feb. 18, 2020. "The Ballooning Costs of Long-Term Care."
https://www.americanactionforum.org/research/the-ballooning-costs-of-long-term-care/

Do the math and you'll quickly realize not planning for this potential cost could have a devastating impact, not only on your finances, but also those of a surviving spouse. To help illustrate this to my clients, I use software showing the cost of care today; the projected cost in the future, including inflation; the potential cost per month; and how these costs, if incurred, will affect a client's financial plan.

How does one plan to pay for such care should it become necessary?

Some retirees with a significant amount of assets may be able to self-fund long-term care from their retirement portfolios. But even these people know, when you start withdrawing money from a retirement portfolio for long-term care, it can reduce your assets at an alarming rate.

This is especially true if you plan to sell red money (at-risk growth assets) to finance long-term care. As we discussed earlier in this chapter, I repeat: When selling such assets during a market downturn, you are forced to sell more shares at a lower price to generate your needed income. Then you have fewer shares available for any possible market recovery, a situation that could leave a surviving spouse or other loved ones in a very serious financial bind.

You need to address the potential for long-term care costs long before this prospect becomes a reality. Again, assigning a specific purpose to a certain portion of your assets (in this case, paying for long-term care) makes sense. You might do this by putting money in any investment(s) not subject to sequence risk or large market-related drawdowns. This kind of planning provides a better chance you will have the money you need when you need it most. Equally crucial, it can help protect your portfolio, your retirement plan, and, most notably, your spouse or family.

HANDLING LONGEVITY RISK

We all aspire to live a long, healthy life. Personally, I believe reducing stress though the creation of a sound retirement plan is one way to improve our chances of achieving this goal.

Longevity arrives with risks, however, that might not be readily apparent. For example, no one knows how long they will live. We do know life expectancy is steadily rising, however. Many people are now retired for twenty, thirty, or even forty years. While wonderful, it is something for which you must prepare.

As the years pass by, you will experience many good times but, history tells us, there will also be challenges. The products we buy will grow more expensive, health care costs will likely rise, tax laws may change, and the stock market will experience ups and downs. Historically, the overall market experiences a downturn every six to eight years. Over the course of a thirty-year retirement, that could mean five market downturns. What we don't know is when these market downturns will happen, how severe they will be, or how long they will last.

Health care costs are also rising each year, so it is reasonable to assume these services will cost more in twenty years than now. Bottom line, we don't know exactly what the future will look like or how long our retirements will last.

One way to think of longevity is as a multiplier of all other risks. Think about it: the longer you live, the more likely there will be a market correction, hyper-inflation, rising interest rates, increased health care costs, higher tax rates, etc. If you don't plan for this multiplier, you could be left wondering where your retirement money went.

THE NUMBERS DON'T LIE

When the rubber meets the road, the numbers dictate your options. Your risk tolerance helps indicate what kinds of investments you should consider, but, if the returns from those investments don't meet your retirement goals, your income needs will likely not be met.

For example, if the level of risk you are comfortable with manages your investments at a 4 percent return and you need to realize an 8 percent return to meet your retirement expenses and lifestyle dreams, your income needs aren't going to be met. A professional might then encourage you to be more aggressive with your investment strategy by taking on more risk in order to create the potential for earning a greater return. If taking more risk isn't an option you are comfortable with, then the discussion will turn to how you can earn more money, or spend less, in order to align your needs more closely with your resources.

How are you going to structure your income flow during retirement? The answer to this question dictates how you determine your risk tolerance. If the numbers say you need to be more aggressive with your investing or modify your lifestyle, it becomes a choice you need to make.

CHAPTER FOUR

Creating a Retirement Income Plan

Retirement should be some of the best years of our lives. We should look forward to the years when we no longer *have* to work, exploring options we didn't have time for while employed.

Free from long hours at work, the daily commute, and the stress of dealing with a demanding boss or uncooperative co-workers, retirement will bring the opportunity to do the things that are most important to **you**. You may choose to spend more time with family, visit your grandkids more, take up a hobby or travel. With a little planning and ambition, your retirement years can be incredibly rewarding.

Your life will be a bit different and many of those changes will be welcomed. However, a key component in helping you reach this point in life will be missing: your paycheck. This is perhaps the most dramatic indicator of the transition from the accumulation phase of our life to the distribution phase that is retirement.

The income you earned throughout years of hard work has paid for most everything you now own and has supported the lifestyle you've chosen. Your regular wage earnings not only covered your monthly bills, but they also paid for your home, car, health care, vacations, children's education, clothing, personal care, pets, and whatever other lifestyle elements you chose to maintain.

But when you think about retirement, I would encourage you to regard a slightly different perspective.

Yes, you will be retiring "from" work and all of the challenges of earning a living, but what are you retiring "to"? You've put in your time, worked hard, saved a little money, and you're ready to move on to your next adventure. What does that look like for you?

Perhaps you have a few travel destinations on your bucket list. Europe? Asia? Australia? Maybe you'd like to travel a little closer to home. How about the Grand Canyon or the Redwood Forest? Or maybe you want to spend time at your favorite beach. Perhaps your vision for the future involves simply attending dance recitals and sporting events for your grandkids or just spoiling them a little more. Maybe you'd simply like to host more Sunday dinners for family and friends.

In addition to whatever you would like to do in retirement, you will also want to maintain your current lifestyle without worrying about having enough income to pay your monthly bills. The challenge in retirement is finding a way to pay for all the things you want to do in addition to addressing your regular living expenses—all without receiving a regular paycheck. Finding a way to do this is something often overlooked by many investment advisors, brokers, and retirees.

Sure, you've saved and planned with these types of retirement expenses in mind. You contributed to a 401(k), 403(b), IRA, or a brokerage account and invested for growth. You did so hoping such investments would grow enough to allow you to retire. It was a good plan, and it helped you reach your destination.

However, when you approach or reach retirement, your goal is no longer just to retire—you're already there. Now you need to cover regular household expenses, provide for future medical care, fund your bucket list, and support your lifestyle with income lasting throughout your lifetime and even beyond for surviving spouses and loved ones.

Now it's time to find ways to put the savings you've worked hard to accumulate to work for *you*. Now you want those savings to generate a stable, dependable retirement income stream, capable of supplying financial security in addition to paying all you want to do.

Utility companies, medical providers, airlines, cruise ships, hotels, restaurants, and golf pro shops won't accept shares of your mutual funds as payment. You will need cash and sources of income to produce it. This is where many people who had the foresight to save and invest for their retirement fall short in the retirement income planning phase.

One of the true challenges of retirement planning is knowing how and when to turn retirement savings into retirement income. For many people with retirement investments, this involves selling shares of equity assets to generate cash. This was always part of their plan, no doubt, but keep in mind our discussion from the previous chapter about the risks to your nest egg when selling shares during inevitable market downturns.

INCOME IS KING IN RETIREMENT

Look, I know I said this before, but I will say it again. You need income for retirement, and you must provide it yourself—typically from the retirement assets you've amassed. Attempting to sell investments and take withdrawals from red money/at-risk investments presents a risky proposition. To me, it makes more sense to generate a stream of dependable income from at least a portion of a retirement portfolio that produces regular interest and dividends. A foundation of yellow money assets is essential for this.

Shortly I will show an example of how to reposition a retirement portfolio to better accomplish this goal.

The amount of income you will need in retirement is mostly up to you. It will be based on your lifestyle, your regular living expenses, and your personal "bucket list." There are major exceptions, of course—medical expenses over which we have little to no control of can impact even the best-prepared plan—but, for now, let's focus on what we can control. Some of my clients want a simple retirement lifestyle keeping them close to home. Others want to travel the world. Some want to spend all their savings during retirement, while others want to leave as much as possible to their loved ones. Retirement is personal and should be about what *you* want. Consequently, there is no "one size fits all" plan.

There is, however, one common bond we all share: wanting a financially secure future. You can't count on hoping you'll buy a winning lottery ticket, but you can certainly build a solid foundation by starting with an established stream of income satisfying (and hopefully exceeding) your projected regular retirement expenses.

The first aim in creating an income plan should be satisfying your regular financial obligations. Your living expenses are what they are, and you'll need to pay them before you do anything else.

Fortunately, living expenses in retirement are usually different from what we knew earlier in life. Those were the years when we had dependent children who required food (lots of it), education, and recreation; when we had rent or mortgage payments to make; or maybe even college loans to repay. Yet even in retirement, there are utility bills, ever-present taxes, emergency needs such as home repairs, and likely rising medical costs that become regular expenses. You might even find you are still helping your children make their way.

After accounting for routine expenses, your income plan must account for the fun stuff, the retirement dreams like travel, or hobbies, or more time with family and friends, or putting money aside for your grandkids' college education.

After you've budgeted for those things, you have an idea of how much income you're going to need in retirement. Once you know that, you can look at what you have in assets and explore how to turn those into income that can help you achieve your goals.

Needless to say, if your assets aren't sufficient to support your needs and goals, you may need to consider more aggressive investments to pursue higher returns, allocate more of your savings to generating income, trim your budget, or even consider a part-time job.

You may also find yourself in a better financial position than you originally thought. I have many clients who have been able to make positive adjustments to their retirement plan because we were able to generate more income than they needed, thus enabling them to take an extra vacation or two each year while maintaining the financial security that they require.

Income can be produced in a lot of ways in retirement. Social Security is the foundational source for most people, and since it is so important, I will spend the entire next chapter talking about it. Income can also be produced from real estate, pensions, investments and—whether you *must* do this, or merely *want* to—part-time employment.

Keep in mind, Social Security typically does not fill all income needs for most retired people, though some (unfortunately) are completely dependent on it for all income. For those with other options, however, we'll spend Chapter 6 talking about ways to fill what is commonly called "the income gap" between what Social Security provides and what an individual's need might be.

Let's conclude this section by considering a question I often ask during the educational workshops I offer:

Can you tell me how much income/dividends/interest your portfolio earned last year?

You can probably guess that most people can't answer this question accurately. I don't mean to criticize, but if you want to begin real retirement income planning, this is something you need to know.

Establishing an efficient, comprehensive retirement income plan that meets your basic income needs is the best way I know of helping achieve your lifestyle dreams. It helps you manage your risk expectations for your other investments, helps in legacy planning, and can help reduce the stress level common to people who worry they will live longer than their money.

REPOSITIONING ASSETS TO PRODUCE ADDITIONAL INCOME

A strategy I often employ with clients looking to turn their retirement assets into income involves repositioning those assets into more income-friendly financial products. This strategy can be used not only in an attempt to increase income, but also to reduce some of the volatility of market-exposed assets.

Let's take a look at how this strategy might work.

John and Mary Smith are mythical clients with the very real-world situation of wanting a solid income plan to maintain their lifestyle after they stop working. They have just reached full retirement age and are ready to start enjoying life. They saved what they could for retirement and are preparing to make the big move with steady income from Social Security and a small pension Mary will receive from a former employer.

Their current retirement incomes picture looks like this:

- John's Social Security at full retirement age: $2,600 monthly
- Mary's Social Security at full retirement age: $1,400 monthly
- Mary's pension: $320 monthly for life with full survivor benefit
- Total income from Social Security: $4,000 monthly/$48,000 annually
- Total income from pension: $320 monthly/$3,840 annually

Total existing benefit income: $4,320 monthly/$51,840 annually

John and Mary have calculated they need $8,000 per month ($96,000 annually) in gross income (before taxes) to cover their living expenses and maintain their current lifestyle. In addition, they would like to take a nice extended vacation each year, as well as visit their out-of-state grandchildren. They have calculated that these travel expenses will cost $12,000 each year.

When including travel along with their daily living expenses, they have calculated they need retirement income of $108,000 per year, or $9,000 per month.

As noted above, the Smiths expect to receive $51,840 annually from their existing benefits from Social Security and Mary's pension. These benefits clearly do not meet their income needs, and they plan to fill this gap by withdrawing what is needed from their retirement accounts.

John and Mary worked hard to save money and grow their retirement assets. They are invested in a very common portfolio, approximately 80 percent of which is in mutual funds, which I consider to be "red money" assets. Most of these mutual funds are stock funds. Others are bond mutual funds, but they are all exposed to market risk. In addition to the mutual funds, they own a few common stocks, two CDs, and a few money market funds as well as a savings account that holds their emergency funds.

Both John and Mary are concerned about market volatility and would like to reduce their risk, but they also know they need to invest some of their money for growth if they want it to last throughout retirement.

Below is a list of their retirement assets:
- John's 401(k): $732,000
- Mary's IRA: $206,000
- John's Roth IRA: $32,000
- Mary's Roth IRA: $68,000
- Joint brokerage account: $164,000

Total: $1,202,000

The Smiths also own their home, which has a current market value of $400,000.

Evaluating this portfolio for the purpose of building a retirement income plan, let's first break the investments into red, yellow and green "buckets."

For the purpose of this example, their combined investments break down as follows:
- Red money assets: $926,000
- Yellow money assets: $62,000
- Green money assets: $214,000

Total: $1,202,000

After breaking down the investments, it is helpful to determine how much income the portfolio is generating. Remember, income is determined by the interest and dividends that the investments are generating. Income is **not** capital appreciation or the increase in the present-day value of the investments.

You may be wondering why I don't consider growth or capital appreciation to be income. That's a great question but one that also has a simple answer: Capital appreciation is not something that we can count on. The value of investments literally changes by the minute. "Gains" made in the morning can evaporate by lunchtime. It is my opinion that your income stream should be far more dependable and predictable, and my clients seem to agree.

So, how much income might these assets produce in retirement to offset any gap between Social Security and Mary's pension income and their total needs? Let's take a look at the income produced by the assets currently in the Smiths' portfolio:

Current Income		
Assets	**Average Yield**	**Projected Annual Income**
Red money $926,000	1.32%	$12,223
Yellow money $62,000	3.51%	$2,176
Green money $214,000	0.86%	$1,840
Total projected income (interest and dividends) from all investments: $16,239 annually/$1,353 monthly		

John and Mary's projected income shortfall:

• Estimated total annual expenses (including travel): $108,000 annually/$9,000 monthly

• Total income from all sources (Social Security, pension, interest and dividends from retirement assets): $68,079 annually/$5,673 monthly

Income shortfall: $39,921 annually/$3,326 monthly

This shortfall means, with their current investment strategy, the Smiths will have to withdraw over $3,300 from their retirement nest egg each and every month during retirement. That number is likely to increase over time as prices rise due to inflation. Their investments are not generating enough income through dividends and interest to support their needs, so each month they will have to sell some shares of their mutual funds or stocks to generate the cash needed to meet their estimated expenses. Over the course of a twenty-, twenty-five- or thirty-year retirement, there will be many such withdrawals.

Keep in mind too, that during retirement, they won't be making contributions to their 401(k) or IRA accounts, which means they won't be buying additional shares every two weeks as they did while working. Every month in retirement, when they sell shares and take withdrawals, they end up with fewer shares. Does that sound like a good plan to you? It sure doesn't to me.

Put another way, they are dipping into their retirement nest egg each month as they have to sell an undetermined number of shares to cover their expenses. They will sell when the market is up as well as when it is down. Does anybody really want to sell their investments when their value is down?

Let's think about that for a minute.

John and Mary have done a great job with their accounts and are in the enviable position of having over $1.2 million in retirement savings.

Yet, they have an income goal that exceeds the combined income from their Social Security, pension, interest, and dividends. They will be forced to dip into their principal and make difficult decisions when they have to sell some of their shares each month to support their lifestyle.

Our hypothetical John and Mary would likely not be comfortable with this strategy due to its many unknowns. Most people in similar positions want more control over their retirement income streams and have the freedom to make good financial decisions in regard to managing their investments. So, for John and Mary, we'd look at making a few changes to their strategy and focus a bit more on a few factors that, in my experience, are the most important to the majority of people I work with.

Those factors are:
• Lowering risk
• Generating retirement income
• Maintaining principal

These factors actually can work hand in hand while still providing an opportunity for growth. How? It's actually quite simple. Common sense, an open mind, and a clear vision of what's most important to **your** financial future are all that is required to start putting together a retirement income strategy that meets your needs and gives you the highest probability of achieving those goals.

Let's see what this strategy might look like for John and Mary.

We'll start by reallocating some of their retirement savings in order to 1) generate more income through interest and dividends, and 2) lower their risk exposure to market volatility.

John and Mary Reallocations		
	Old	*New*
Red Money	$926,000	$400,000
Yellow Money	$62,000	$400,000
Green Money	$214,000	$400,000

By lowering the amount held in red-money investments and reallocating those funds into both yellow and green investments, we can achieve our goal of lowering exposure to market risk.

Our other goal is to generate more retirement income. This can be done using any number of different strategies or products, but the goal is to increase yield by investing specifically to earn interest and dividends so your money is working as hard as you did to generate income.

This is an example of what the reallocated portfolio could look like, plus the income it might generate:

Reallocated Income						
	Old Balance	*Old Yield*	*Old Income*	*New Balance*	*New Yield*	*New Income*
Red Money	$926,000	1.32%	$12,233	$400,000	3.25%	$13,000
Yellow Money	$62,000	3.51%	$2,176	$400,000	5.2%	$20,800
Green Money	$214,000	0.86%	$1,840	$400,000	4.2%	$16,800
		Old Total Income	**$16,239**		**New Total Income**	**$50,600**

The new allocation has the potential to generate over $34,000 more in income, hopefully without draining the principal. It also lowers exposure to market risk and greatly enhances the likelihood that the Smiths will be able to maintain their principal.

How did we get to this position of increased revenue potential? Without getting too deep into the weeds, let's note simply that we moved approximately $526,000 from at-risk, red money assets into income-producing yellow and green money assets (to review examples of what is in each category, revisit Chapter Two).

After repositioning funds into green and yellow money investments to generate income, we then return to our red, or growth, investments. I believe that income is an invaluable piece to a retirement investment strategy, so in addition to considering the growth potential for our red money investments, we may also look to increase the yield or dividends that these investments can generate.

MAKE DECISIONS WHEN YOU *WANT* TO, NOT BECAUSE YOU *HAVE* TO

Additionally, because the dividends and interest now being generated exceed John and Mary's income need, they won't have to sell any of their investments unless they choose to do so, which will help them maintain their principal for the rest of their lives. This can help them have the cash to leave a legacy for their beneficiaries or perhaps assist with health care or long-term care costs later in life.

Another aspect of this strategy will present itself when John and Mary must begin taking required minimum distributions (RMDs) from tax-qualified accounts such as their IRAs, 401(k)s, and 403(b)s. The interest and dividends can be distributed when earned, which will help satisfy this requirement without the need to sell investments each year to meet this IRS requirement. We will look at RMDs in more detail in Chapter Nine, "Taxes and Retirement."

The preceding figures are projections only and offer no guarantee that the Smiths can actually more than triple their annual retirement investment income (from approximately $16,000 to more than $50,000) after repositioning assets. They do illustrate, however, the potential significance of income-producing assets.

The bottom line here is to take a big-picture look at your retirement assets and how they can be converted into income in retirement.

The Smiths may, in fact, have done very well for themselves with their original red money retirement portfolio configuration. At least, when the market is up, they likely would do very well.

But what happens when they need income from red money assets during a market downturn, or with a full-scale correction or bear market?

Relying on assets exposed to market risk to generate income on demand is, in my opinion, a significant gamble in retirement. The strategy may work, or it may not. Most of the people I meet with are not comfortable with a "maybe" when building a retirement plan, so I like to do things the old-fashioned way. Invest first in good companies and strategies that earn interest and dividends to satisfy your income needs, meet RMDs, and limit volatility. Then by all means, consider growth investments with any funds that aren't needed specifically to generate income.

CHAPTER FIVE

Understanding Social Security

Most Americans rely on income from Social Security benefits during retirement. For some, it is the primary source of retirement income. For too many, sadly, it is the sole source.

Given the important role Social Security plays in the lives of most retired Americans, examining your benefit options is one of the first steps a financial professional will take in creating your retirement income plan. These benefits are, after all, the foundation of income planning for most retirees, and a reliable source of green money.

Many people know at least the basics of Social Security; that is, that you've paid into the Social Security Trust Fund through payroll withholding (FICA taxes) throughout your working life, and at some time around retirement age, Uncle Sam owes you a pension.

But Social Security isn't that easy. When it comes time for you to cash in on your Social Security benefit—your government-sponsored pension—you will have many options and choices, just as you do with most pension plans available in the private or public sector.

These decisions will have a lifetime effect on the benefit you will receive each month. Experts have spent their entire careers understanding and analyzing Social Security options. Entire books have been written on the subject, and this book does not purport to be one of them.

Luckily, you don't have to understand all of Social Security's intricacies to make it work for you. You do, however, need to know your options when determining how to make the most of your personal Social Security benefit.

Here are two basic concepts I consider essential in your understanding of how to best manage your benefit.

First is the concept of full retirement age (FRA) and the understanding that the full benefit to which you are entitled will be paid upon reaching this age. Your FRA is set by the SSA and might be different than the year you actually retire. For most readers of this book, FRA is likely to be either sixty-six or sixty-seven (or some point in-between) depending on year of birth. A chart later in this chapter will provide a full year-by-year breakdown as we discuss FRA in more detail.

The second essential is knowing that, though you are eligible to receive Social Security's retired worker benefits as early as age sixty-two, taking them before your FRA will reduce your monthly benefit by a fraction of a percent for every month prior to FRA. Moreover, this reduction is permanent.[4] It establishes a baseline that stays with you for the rest of your life, and the amount of your benefit will increase only when cost-of-living adjustments (COLAs) are applied. On a more positive note, filing for benefits after your FRA can increase your benefit check for life. More on this later.

Both factors will affect your decision on when to begin taking Social Security, as that decision will affect your ability to get the most from your benefits. Taking the time to create a roadmap for your Social Security strategy will help ensure you are able to exact your maximum benefit and efficiently coordinate it with the rest of your retirement plan.

We need to note here before going further that, when referring to "Social Security" in this book, we will be talking exclusively about the "retired worker benefit" built upon a person's work history, as opposed to the Social Security Disability Insurance (SSDI) available to disabled Americans or getting into options for those caring for minors.

---

[4] *It is possible to change your mind after making your decision on taking benefits, but your ability to do so depends on your age. A person receiving benefits before reaching FRA can, within twelve months of starting, petition the Social Security Administration to stop receiving benefits. Such a decision requires repaying the Social Security Administration all benefits received to that point, as well as any spousal or children's benefits based on your record. A person who has reached FRA or later can elect to voluntarily suspend benefits without a repayment penalty. This is a one-time only option.* Source: "If you change your mind." Social Security Administration, https://www.ssa.gov/planners/retire/withdrawal.html

There are many aspects of Social Security over which you have no control. You don't control how much you put into it, and you don't control how the government manages it.

However, you do control when and how you file for benefits. Consequently, the biggest question you must ask and answer about Social Security is, "When should I start taking it?" Keep in mind when addressing this issue that the decision you make not only permanently affects the monthly benefit you will receive for the rest of your life, but it also establishes a baseline that determines the benefit available to a spouse. (We'll discuss spousal benefits and survivor benefits in greater detail later in this chapter.)

A CLOSER LOOK AT SOCIAL SECURITY BASICS

Before we get into a few calculations and strategies that can make a significant difference in making the most of your benefit, let's first cover some basic information about Social Security to give you a better idea of how to prepare for it.

Full Retirement Age. FRA is an essential figure for anyone planning to receive Social Security and is dictated by your year of birth. Again, you are entitled to your full work-history benefit upon reaching FRA. Taking benefits either before (beginning as early as age 62) or after reaching FRA can have a negative or positive effect, respectively, on that benefit. We'll examine those negative and positive effects in more detail here shortly.

When Social Security was initially established in 1935 as part of the recovery from the Great Depression, one idea was that it could incentivize older workers to step away from their jobs to create opportunities for younger workers—the FRA was age sixty-five, and it still is for people born before 1938. But as time passed (and life expectancy increased), the age for receiving full retirement benefits increased. Increasing the FRA is one way the government attempted to reduce the cost of the Social Security program.[5]

---

[5] Social Security Administration. "Full Retirement Age."
https://www.ssa.gov/planners/retire/retirechart.html

Social Security FRA	
Year of Birth	*Full Retirement Age*
1943-1954	66
2955	66 and 2 months
1956	66 and 4 months
1957	66 and 6 months
1958	66 and 8 months
1959	66 and 10 months
1960 or later	67

Spousal benefit. If you are at least sixty-two years old and have been married to a recipient of Social Security benefits for at least twelve months, you can choose to receive a spousal benefit even if you do not have the minimum forty credits required to begin drawing benefits based on your own work history.

This spousal benefit is generally one half of that earned by the spouse who is actively receiving benefits. Note that at least one spouse in a couple must currently be receiving benefits before a spousal benefit can be taken by the other partner. Note too that the amount of benefit established when the working spouse first started taking benefits establishes a permanent baseline for spousal benefits, meaning if someone takes their benefit before FRA, it decreases the potential spousal benefit as well.

Now let's now look at how your benefit is determined.

Primary Insurance Amount. You can think of your Primary Insurance Amount (PIA) like a ripening fruit. It represents the amount of your Social Security benefit at your full retirement age, the point at which your benefit becomes fully ripe. (The formula for computing PIA is complex, but you can learn more about it on the Social Security website at https://www.ssa.gov/oact/cola/piaformula.html)

If, however, you opt to begin taking benefits before your FRA, you are picking a fruit before it is ripe, and your monthly benefit will be less than your PIA. Technically, the reduction rate is 5/9 of 1 percent for the first thirty-six months in which benefits are taken before FRA. If that "early" period exceeds thirty-six months, the reduction rate becomes 5/12 of 1 percent for each additional month.

In more understandable terms, the SSA says a person with an FRA of sixty-six can expect a 25 percent reduction in monthly benefit if that benefit is first taken at age sixty-two, four full years before FRA. A person with an FRA of sixty-seven can expect a 30 percent reduction if benefits are first taken at sixty-two, five full years before FRA.[6]

On a more positive note, waiting until after your FRA to begin taking benefits will increase that benefit beyond your PIA. By using what are known as "delayed retirement credits," most readers of this book—that is anyone born in 1943 or later—can increase their benefit by 8 percent each year (or a fraction thereof in a partial year) by electing to delay taking benefits until after FRA. Delayed retirement credits end at age seventy, and a benefit will not increase—other than through cost of living adjustments—after that.

DECIDING NOW OR LATER

Even though Social Security is the foundation of most people's retirement income, too many Americans fail to realize the total impact it can have on the overall viability of a retirement plan.

To put this in a different perspective, consider every dollar you can get from Social Security income means less money you will have to take from your retirement nest egg to meet your income needs. The difference between the best and worst Social Security decision can be tens of thousands of dollars over a lifetime of benefits.

Following the preceding logic, it makes sense to wait as long as you can to begin receiving your Social Security benefit, right? Unfortunately, that isn't an option for everyone.

Not everyone can afford to wait, and for others it doesn't make sense to wait for one reason or another. Many people need to rely on Social Security on Day One of their retirement; they need the income right now. Others might be in poor health and don't think they will live long enough to make waiting until FRA or beyond worthwhile.

---

[6] "Social Security Benefits: Early or Late Retirement."
https://www.ssa.gov/OACT/quickcalc/early_late.html

However, I suspect many who take an early benefit are simply under-informed about Social Security, and make this major decision based on bad information, misguided friendly suggestions, or emotion.

Here is an instance where consulting with a financial professional might be beneficial. Financial professionals have access to software that can help you determine the best year and month for you to file for benefits based on your default life expectancy. You can further customize that information by estimating your life expectancy based on knowledge of your own health, living habits, and family history.

How can you calculate your life expectancy? Well, none of us know exactly how long we'll live, but you likely have a better idea than the government does. You have much more personal information about your health, lifestyle, and family history than the government actuaries who rely on averages to make their life expectancy calculations.

After using your personal knowledge to make your educated guess about life expectancy, you and your advisor can then discuss the state of your other retirement savings assets, which also will play a huge role in your decision about when to begin taking Social Security.

GEORGE AND MARY BAILEY WANT A WONDERFUL LIFE

Let's take a look at a hypothetical example that shows the impact of working with a financial professional to optimize Social Security benefits.

George and Mary Bailey—yes, the same names as the fictional couple from the Christmas classic "It's a Wonderful Life"—have worked their whole lives and saved and invested when they could. For the purpose of simplicity, let's say both are fifty-nine years old and were born a few months apart in 1960, meaning their full retirement age is sixty-seven. They'll soon be eligible for Social Security at age sixty-two, and they want to explore their options several years before having the first opportunity to make a decision.

Sitting down with their long-time financial professional, they explored the Social Security website—though they didn't need a professional to do this—and learned their monthly benefits at FRA were $1,900 for George and $900 for Mary. That would give them $2,800 a month, or $33,600 a year, if both wait until their FRA to file for benefits.

But George and Mary have long-standing dreams of retiring early, enjoying more of life outside the work force while they can. They look at their options if taking benefits at sixty-two, five years before FRA, and learn from the SSA website that both their monthly benefits will be reduced by 30 percent if taken at the first possible opportunity. George's monthly benefit would be reduced from $1,900 at FRA to $1,330, and Mary's from $900 to $630. Their monthly income would be $1,960 and their annual income $23,520.

A significant decrease, but one partially offset by the knowledge that they will receive sixty Social Security paychecks—twelve monthly checks (albeit at a lower amount in each) every year for five years—before they would see a larger amount in each monthly check at FRA.

But, as we noted above, the Baileys saved and invested during their working years. Perhaps they had some inheritance money as well, or could supplement income with part-time work. For whatever reason, they decided to explore the idea of taking benefits a bit later and using their retirement assets for income until age seventy when their Social Security benefits would grow to their fullest.

George learned from the SSA website that his monthly benefit would increase from $1,900 at FRA to $2,356 after three years growth at 8 percent annually. If Mary also waited to age seventy, her monthly benefit after the 24 percent cumulative hike would rise to $1,116. At age seventy, the Baileys could realize $3,472 each month and $41,664 a year. Their monthly paychecks would grow considerably, but they also would be receiving thirty-six fewer checks than at FRA and ninety-six fewer than at age sixty-two.

Note here that a person isn't obligated to take Social Security at age seventy. Possible reasons for not doing so might include having enough available wealth that a person does not want to take on the tax liability of additional income from Social Security. But, because delayed retirement credits end at age seventy, most people who delay taking benefits beyond their FRA begin taking them once they max out. To not do so is essentially leaving money on the table.

Let's take a side-by-side look at the comparisons.

THE BAILEYS AT FRA (67)

(Note: Cost-of-living adjustments are not included in these examples)
- George: $1,900/month, or $22,800/year
- Mary: $900/month, or $10,800/year
- Total for the Baileys at FRA: $2,800/month, or $33,600/year

THE BAILEYS AT EARLIEST OPPORTUNITY (62)

(Early means minus 30 percent for each)
- George: $1,330/month, or $15,960/year
- Mary: $630/month, or $7,560/year
- Total for the Baileys at 62: $1,960/month, or $23,520/year

BAILEYS WITH DELAYED RETIREMENT CREDITS (70)

(Delayed means plus 24 percent for each)
- George: $2,356/month, or $28,272/year
- Mary: $1,116/month, or $13,392/year
- Total for the Baileys at 70: $3,472/month, or $41,664/year

Now let's stretch those amounts over a few hypothetical timelines.

Let's assume George and Mary reach age eighty. What will their total take from Social Security look like at this point when viewed in the three different scenarios—"early filing," FRA, and "delayed filing? Keep in mind that in the early filing example (age sixty-two) the couple has been receiving reduced payments for eighteen years while they will have thirteen years of full PIA payments in the FRA example (age sixty-seven) and only ten years of enhanced payments in the delayed filing case (at age seventy).

Following is how the Social Security benefit totals might look for the couple at age eighty under each of the preceding scenarios.

TOTAL SOCIAL SECURITY BENEFITS AT AGE 80		
(Note: Cost-of-living adjustments not included)		
Filing Age	Years Receiving Benefits	Total Lifetime Payments
62	18	$423,360 at $23,520/year
FRA	13	$446,800 at $33,600/year
70	10	$416,640 at $41,664/year

The advantage in total benefits here clearly goes to the FRA decision, but even the "early option" has an edge over the "late option" at this point. So, what's the big deal about trying to wait until age seventy? Let's extend our timeline another two years for an answer.

TOTAL SOCIAL SECURITY BENEFITS AT AGE 82		
(Note: Cost-of-living adjustments not included)		
Filing Age	Years Receiving Benefits	Total Lifetime Payments
62	20	$470,400 at $23,520/year
FRA	15	$504,000 at $33,600/year
70	12	$499,968 at $41,664/year

The edge still goes to the FRA decision, but the late option has now passed the early choice by nearly $30,000. That gap will become even more pronounced if the Baileys live another three years.

TOTAL SOCIAL SECURITY BENEFITS AT AGE 85		
(Note: Cost-of-living adjustments not included)		
Filing Age	Years Receiving Benefits	Total Lifetime Payments
62	23	$540,960 at $23,520/year
FRA	18	$604,800 at $33,600/year
70	15	$624,960 at $41,664/year

Now the edge clearly goes to the age seventy decision above all the others. There is an $84,000 difference here between the full amount of delayed retirement credits and the benefits created when taken at the earliest possible opportunity.

Clearly, the advantage in Social Security goes to those with longevity, but who among us is guaranteed that? This is the question one must decide, the gamble one takes, when making the decision on when to first begin taking benefits either on a reduced, full, or enhanced basis. There is no right answer for everyone but knowing something of both the short- and long-term prospects gives you a basis for a better-informed decision.

This is why the choice is up to you and you alone.

There's no telling how much you could miss out on from your Social Security if you don't take time to look up your PIA and then create a strategy that calculates your maximum benefit. For the Baileys, the value of making the most of their benefits was the difference between night and day. While this may seem like a special case, it isn't uncommon to find benefit increases of this magnitude. You'll never know unless you take a look at your own options.

One final point. Don't expect much in the way of guidance from your Uncle Sam in making this decision. While helpful representatives at your local or regional SSA offices are available to answer specific questions, "When is the best time for me to begin taking Social Security?" is not one of them. Yes, they can tell you what your monthly benefit will be at FRA, and even compute the amount if taken earlier or later than FRA. They can outline the basic options as I've done here. But they are prohibited from giving specific advice when it comes to the all-important question of how to maximize lifetime benefit income.

TYPES OF SOCIAL SECURITY BENEFITS:

• Retired Worker Benefit. This is the benefit we've been discussing to this point, the one with which most people are familiar. Sometimes generically called the "work-history benefit," the Retired Worker Benefit is what most people are talking about when they refer to Social Security. It is your benefit based on your earnings and the amount that you have paid into the system over the span of your career.

• Spousal benefit. This is available to a spouse of someone who is receiving a Retired Worker Benefit. This benefit is designed to provide a safety net pension protection for people without a prolonged history of workplace employment. A perfect example are people who worked only part-time, or homemakers whose lifetime of hard, stay-at-home work in raising a family, is never rewarded with a paycheck. The spousal benefit provides the opportunity to receive a Social Security check that can be as much as 50 percent of the check at FIA of a primary earner who is actively receiving benefits.

There are aspects to filing for spousal benefits that can be complicated. Seeking the guidance of a professional with a solid knowledge of Social Security isn't always necessary but can be helpful when considering what are known as "spousal coordination strategies" that can help maximize a couple's combined Social Security benefits.

With that in mind, let's look at some basics of spousal benefits.[7]

A full spousal benefit—50 percent of the benefit of the spouse actively taking a Retired Worker Benefit—is available only when the person seeking the spousal benefit has reached FRA.

Though you are eligible to begin taking a spousal benefit at age sixty-two, that benefit will be reduced from the full benefit at FRA.

As a spousal benefit is based on the Retired Worker Benefit being actively taken by a (typically) higher-earning spouse, a decision by the primary earner to take an early-filing/reduced benefit also permanently reduces the size of the spousal benefit available.[8]

Though a higher-earning spouse eligible for a Retired Worker Benefit can delay filing until after FRA—thus growing their benefit by 8 percent a year through delayed retirement credits—a spousal benefit does not experience this growth. A spousal benefit can never be more than half of the Retired Worker Benefit at its FRA level.

Sometimes a spousal benefit taken at FRA is higher than a person's work-history benefit. In that case, the person filing for benefits is

---

[7] Social Security Administration, "Benefits for Your Spouse."
https://www.ssa.gov/planners/retire/applying6.html

[8] *In a vast majority of cases, spousal benefits are taken by a lower-earning spouse based on the benefit being actively taken by the higher-earning member of the couple. But it is possible for a higher earner who is eligible to file a restricted application— that is, who was born before January 2, 1954—to file for a spousal benefit based on the benefit of the lower-earning spouse. The higher earner could then let his or her own work-history benefit grow until age seventy, at which time a switch would be made to the higher earner's enhanced work-history benefit.*

automatically given the highest possible benefit—a change from previous options, such as the "restricted application."

• Survivor benefit. When a person who is eligible for Social Security benefits passes away, a surviving spouse who is at least age sixty (with some exceptions we'll discuss in a bit) is eligible to receive the larger of the two benefits available to the couple. The smaller of the couple's two benefits then disappears.

Survivor benefits have some interesting bells and whistles that are not available with other benefits. Getting professional help can assist a surviving spouse in receiving much-needed assistance at the worst time of many people's lives—that is, immediately after the loss of a husband or wife. A key factor in many of these options, as it is with all matters dealing with Social Security, is the full retirement age of the survivor and the deceased as well as the filing status of both.

At least one aspect of survivor benefits offers an option that is not generally available with spousal benefits. Specifically, a surviving spouse who has not yet filed for benefits may find that a survivor benefit based on the PIA of the deceased is either close in value or even larger than their own work-history benefit. In such cases, the surviving spouse has the opportunity to take the survivor benefit and let their own Retired Worker Benefit grow until a later time, at which point they can switch to their own now-enhanced personal benefit.

Moreover, a deceased spouse did not have to be actively taking benefits at the time of death in order for a surviving spouse to be eligible for a survivor benefit.

Let's say our fictional George Bailey did not file for benefits at his FRA of sixty-six, hoping to someday realize an enhanced benefit. Sadly, he never saw it; he died at age sixty-eight. His wife Mary is now eligible for a survivor benefit equal to what George would have received at the time of his death. If Mary elects to receive the survivor benefit—if it provides greater income than her personal benefit—her personal benefit goes away.

Let's look at some more typical survivor benefits situations.

As noted above, when both members of a couple are actively receiving benefits, a surviving spouse automatically receives the larger of the two benefits available to the couple. The remaining benefit ends. A survivor already receiving benefits does not have the option to choose the survivor benefit while letting a personal benefit grow. That option is available only to survivors who are not yet receiving benefits.

A widow or widower is eligible to receive a full survivor benefit only when taking it at the survivor's FRA. A survivor benefit taken before FRA will be reduced based on a sliding scale between the survivor's FRA and the time of taking the benefit.

Keep in mind the baseline benefit established by a spouse at the time of initially filing for benefits also permanently affects the survivor benefit. This applies to the baseline established by both early/reduced and delayed/enhanced filings. Note however, that the enhanced benefit baseline will never be greater than the level the deceased established at age seventy. (This is another example of how a survivor benefit has an advantage over a spousal one that cannot exceed more than half of the primary earner's benefit at FRA.)

If a benefits-eligible worker dies before reaching FRA without having filed for benefits, a surviving spouse can, by waiting until the survivor's FRA, receive a survivor benefit based on what the deceased would have received at FRA.

A survivor benefit can be taken as early as age fifty if the surviving spouse is disabled and the disability occurred within seven years of a spouse's death. A survivor benefit can be taken at any age by a surviving spouse who is not yet remarried and is providing care for the deceased worker's minor child (under age sixteen). A similar rule applies to a surviving spouse of any age who provides cares for a disabled child.[9]

Dependent parents, those sixty-two years of age or over for whom a deceased worker was providing at least half of their support, can also be eligible for survivor benefits.

THE DIVORCE FACTOR

If you have gone through a divorce, it might affect the retirement benefit to which you are entitled, especially when it comes to the spousal benefit.

---

[9] Social Security Administration, "Survivor Benefits," https://www.ssa.gov/pubs/EN-05-10084.pdf

You read that correctly. A divorced spouse can receive a benefit based on a former spouse's Social Security record, so long as the following conditions are met:

• Their marriage lasted at least ten years; and

• The person filing for divorce benefits is at least age sixty-two, unmarried, and not entitled to a higher Social Security benefit based on his or her own record.[10]

It is important to note here that, like any spousal benefit, a divorced spouse must be at FRA to receive a full spousal benefit. Anything taken before FRA will permanently reduce the size of the monthly Social Security check.

Some other points to note:

• A divorced spouse who remarries generally cannot claim a benefit based on an ex's record unless the second marriage is ended by divorce, death, or annulment.

• If one ex-spouse is eligible for benefits but has not filed to receive them, a former mate can still qualify for a spousal benefit provided the couple has been divorced for two years.

• A divorced person taking a spousal benefit based on the record of an ex does not affect the benefit of the ex or the ex's current spouse, if any, nor will the ex be notified of the filing.

• A divorced spouse born before January 2, 1954, who has reached FRA (sixty-six for people born before 1960) and who has not yet filed for benefits can file a restricted application requesting either a spousal or personal benefit. Divorced people born after the above date who are eligible for a personal work-history benefit as well as a spousal benefit will automatically receive the higher of the two amounts.

• A divorced spouse of a deceased ex can receive the same benefits as the surviving widow or widower provided that their marriage lasted at least ten years.

• A divorced spouse can remarry only after age sixty (fifty if disabled) without affecting the eligibility to receive a survivor benefit.

---

[10] Social Security Administration, "If you are divorced."
https://www.ssa.gov/planners/retire/divspouse.html

• Survivor benefits paid to a divorced spouse do not affect the benefits paid to other survivors receiving benefits based on the deceased's record.

WORKING IN RETIREMENT

There is a potential penalty when continuing to work while taking Social Security benefits before reaching FRA. The Social Security Administration figures, in effect, that if you "retired early" and are still earning wages above a certain limit, you are not really "retired."

But enough of the negativity. Let's address the good news first.

After FRA, a person receiving Social Security benefits can work and earn all the wages they can command without penalty. One will, of course, pay income taxes at one's normal rate on those earnings, and that additional money could affect the rate at which Social Security benefits are taxed. (We'll address the issue of "provisional income" and its effect on Social Security taxes in our Chapter Nine on taxes.)

For people taking early benefits, however, the picture is not so rosy. The SSA has an earnings limit, which in 2019 was $17,640. For any wages earned over that limit, the SSA will withhold $1 in future benefit payments for every $2 earned over the limit. The withholding is done by suspending monthly benefit checks until the penalty amount is reached.

Example. George Bailey began taking Social Security at age sixty-three even though his FRA is sixty-six. George continued working on a part-time basis because 1) he was slowly winding down from the pace of the daily workplace, and 2) he needed the money. George made (for the purpose of simplicity in this example) $27,640 in 2019, his first year of semi-retirement. That's exactly $10,000 above the earnings limit, which means the SSA—upon learning of the excess earnings from George's 2019 tax return—will withhold $5,000 from future benefit payments until the penalty is paid.

That earnings limit increases (with a corresponding decrease in penalty) in the calendar year in which full retirement age is reached. A person can earn up to $46,920 (the 2019 limit) in the calendar year of reaching FRA. (Only wages earned in the months preceding FRA are counted.) The SSA will deduct $1 for every $3 earned over the limit.

Note that a special rule applies to wages earned in a year in which a person first files for benefits. The SSA is allowed to pay a full monthly benefit check in that year for all months it considers you to be fully retired, regardless of yearly earnings.

Now it's time to cheer up. Any money withheld from your benefit check will eventually be repaid upon reaching FRA. The repayment is done through enhanced payments until the repayment amount is reached.

A FEW COMMON MISTAKES

Part of maximizing your Social Security benefit means considering other real-world factors beyond raw numbers. The following mistakes are the result of omitting real-world considerations when planning to file for Social Security benefits.

Underestimating the possibility that you will go back to work. Your retirement is unlike anything else you have ever done. You don't really know what to expect when you get there. Some people love the extra time and freedom, while others miss the purpose and drive of the workplace. If you've filed for Social Security benefits prior to your full retirement age and you decide to go back to work, it could cost you a significant penalty as detailed prior.

Not considering your spouse. The age at which you file for your Social Security benefit can affect your spouse after you pass away. You should take the time to become educated about how your filing decision affects both you and your spouse before you make a final decision.

Taking unprofessional advice. Everyone has an opinion about what you should do regarding Social Security. Your neighbor, your brother-in-law, your friends at work all have stories about what has and what hasn't worked for them or people they know. Someone's father waited until the age of seventy and got a bigger benefit for only a short time before passing, while someone else's mom retired at age sixty-two and enjoyed a long life of benefits. Everyone has a different story to tell.

Your situation, however, is unique to you, and you should make a decision that makes sense for you. This decision should take into consideration your other available retirement assets and work in concert with the other components of your retirement plan. Choosing the most efficient benefit option will help you retain the value of your retirement portfolio and support your income needs. Remember, your Social Security benefit disappears when you pass away, but your assets don't.

With all of the different options, strategies, and benefits to choose from, you can see why filing for Social Security is more complicated than just mailing in the paperwork.

Gathering the data and making yourself aware of all your different options isn't enough to know exactly what to do. However. On the one hand, you can knock yourself out trying to figure out which options are best for you. On the other hand, you can work with a financial professional who uses customized software that takes all the variables of your specific situation into account in helping you calculate your best option.

You have many different options when filing for your Social Security benefit. If your spouse is a different age than you are, it nearly doubles the amount of options you have. This is far more complicated arithmetic than most people can do on their own.

If you want a better understanding of when and how to file, work with someone who will ask you the right questions about your specific situation, someone who has access to specialized software that can crunch the numbers, and who can give you an idea of how Social Security will affect the other pieces of your financial puzzle. The reality is you need to work with a professional who can provide you with a sophisticated analysis of your situation to help you make a truly informed decision.

CHAPTER SIX

Filling the Income Gap

Our time spent in the daily workforce—a period that can account for two-thirds to three-quarters of our lives—is often a hectic, harried time, sometimes called "the rat race." We eagerly look forward to the day we can stop running, only to learn that awaiting us at the end of the race is another challenge: "the retirement cliff."

You stop earning a paycheck at work and start living off of your assets. Some people reach the edge of the cliff and make a slow, controlled, comfortable descent. Others, unfortunately, make a Thelma-and-Louise-like plunge into the canyon.

How you amass and manage your assets and income will determine what kind of transition you make into the retirement phase of life.

Social Security benefits will help in that transition, as will a pension, if you have one. Yet, even with a government or private pension and Social Security, you still may have a difference between your retirement expenses and your retirement income, what is known as "the income gap." Filling that gap is one of the most important parts of a retirement plan.

Ideally, you hope to fill the gap in an efficient manner by using a portion of your retirement assets to establish a stream of income without completely depleting your principal.

Doing all this involves more than just solving a math problem—real life happens. You may, for instance, get a call one day from your grown son asking for help in funding his daughter's college education. Your adult daughter may lose her job and ask for help making a mortgage payment. You might want or need a new car, home improvements, or have the opportunity for an unplanned but much-anticipated foreign vacation with friends. Advance planning can make all the difference between effectively managing all these retirement wants, needs, and opportunities as opposed to plunging out-of-control over the retirement cliff.

We looked at Social Security strategies in the previous chapter and saw how you can have some control over this major component of retirement income based on how and when you file for benefits. We also learned that Social Security alone typically isn't enough to provide all retirement income necessary for many people.

This is where your personal retirement savings come into play. But sometimes even people with such assets fail to examine how they can most efficiently be converted into retirement income.

ANNUITIES: A HYBRID APPROACH TO YOUR INCOME NEEDS

For some people trying to procure a steady income, an annuity may be a good option.

Ask yourself the following questions:

• How concerned are you about finding a financial vehicle that offers the potential to better protect your savings?

• How concerned are you that there may be a better way to actively take income from your savings?

• How concerned are you about finding a tool that offers both income and the potential for growth?

An income annuity can be a good option for addressing income gaps. Because these products are designed for consistent income payments, they may have the same feel as that reliable Social Security benefit check you get every month. Annuity income is also ,sometimes compared to establishing your own personal pension. Most importantly, an income annuity can be an efficient way to help fill your income gap.

Annuities come in all kinds of sizes, shapes, and flavors but they all have certain common traits.

In its simplest form, an annuity is a contract you make with an insurance company to restructure your own payment as an income, paid back to you over time. You put money with the company either through a single-payment premium or a series of payments. The insurance company then invests and grows that money as part of its overall investment program. The company, in turn, has a contractual obligation to pay you income, usually after a defined number of years known as the "accumulation period." That promise to make payments is backed by the claims-paying ability of the insurance company. Depending on how the annuity contract is structured, those income payments can last for the rest of your life. Different kinds of annuities even offer some degree of principal protection, and most offer the potential for interest- or market-related growth.

There are four different categories of annuities: the immediate, the fixed annuity, the variable annuity and the fixed index annuity, Let's take a basic look at each.

THE IMMEDIATE ANNUITY

As you may have guessed, this annuity begins making immediate income payments, often called a single-payment annuity. People sometimes make this single premium payment after receiving an inheritance, or perhaps a rollover of another retirement asset or—dare we suggest it—a lottery win or a legal settlement. The insurance company begins making immediate and regular income payments over a designed period of time. The amount of those payments will generally exceed the amount of principal. This is not a popular annuity by any means because, once the principal amount has been put into the contract, the owner has nearly zero control from that point, and while the income payments will be regular and steady, there's little chance to go back or make changes to the contract terms should one's needs and circumstances change.

THE FIXED ANNUITY

A fixed annuity is a bit like a fancy CD. You make a premium payment to an insurance company that in turn guarantees you a fixed rate of interest for the life of that annuity. After the period of time designated in the annuity contract, you get your principal back along with the interest. A fixed annuity in 2019 typically yields somewhere around 3.5 percent.

THE VARIABLE ANNUITY (VA)

The variable annuity tends to receive the most press attention, and much of it is negative. In fact, most of what people have heard about "annuities" is probably about variable annuities. They were the most popular in a different time—especially in the stock market go-go days of the 1990s when the potential for market-based growth was greater than anything a fixed annuity could produce. Today there are other options available that, in my opinion, are more attractive and suitable for people who are interested in an annuity.

The challenge with variable annuities is two-fold: They don't always do what you would like them to do, and they tend to be quite expensive. This is the only annuity in which the contract holder's principal has the potential to experience both growth *and* loss depending on the performance of the stock market.

This happens because variable annuity premiums are invested in "sub accounts" that operate much the way mutual funds do. Sub accounts consist of multiple equities or commodities with similar traits—large cap companies, small cap companies, technology companies, health care companies, global or emerging market companies, different types of bonds, you name it—just as mutual funds are structured. Moreover, just as mutual funds do, the value of those sub accounts can rise or fall daily depending on the performance of the market. Consequently, the overall account value of the variable annuity—the value that will determine the level of income payments once the annuitant elects to begin receiving them—also can rise or fall on a daily basis.

Again, the potential for account growth once made variable annuities a hot item, especially in the 1990s. But the first decade of the twenty-first century took a lot of shine off the glow of variable annuities. The VA continues to be available today with some measure of future income protection with the option of the "income rider" we will discuss soon.

THE FIXED INDEX ANNUITY (FIA)

The fixed index annuity attempts to combine the best components of the fixed and variable annuity into one package.

The FIA earns credited interest based on the positive performance of a market index such as the S&P 500, Dow Jones Industrial Average, NASDAQ, Russell 2000, or any bond or commodity index. An investor can typically pick the market index to which the annuity will be linked at the time of the FIA purchase. If the market index to which your FIA is linked goes up, your account receives a portion of credited interest linked to that rise. The portion you receive is limited in various ways by caps, spreads or participation rates—options often determined by you but sometimes set by the insurance company issuing the annuity contract.

The insurance companies limit your participation in market growth as a trade-off for the company's protection against loss of invested principal due to market volatility. That's right, in an FIA the insurance company assumes the risk against market-related loss, and its cost for doing so is a limit on the consumer's participation in any market growth.

Let's examine how this protection works.

One of the most attractive qualities of the FIA is something called "annual reset," also referred to as a "ratcheting." It works like this: If the market drops below the index level established when you purchased the FIA, you don't suffer a loss in principal. Instead, the insurance company absorbs it. But if the market goes up, your index level is reset at the new higher level and it will not fall below that. This means you never lose money on your contract value while gaining a portion of market upswings.

This new reset level can be calculated monthly, weekly or even daily, but most annuities are measured annually. In an annual reset, the level of the index when you buy, and the index level one year later (the anniversary date), will determine the amount of loss or gain. You and the insurance company are betting that the market will generally go up over time, but only the insurance company is taking a risk if it does not.

Once again, the insurer's price for assuming all this risk is a limit on the annuitant's participation in any gain. The insurance company retains the difference between any index gain and the annuitant's share of that gain. It might place a "cap" on your share of credited interest, anywhere from 3 to 7 percent of the index growth. In other words, if your linked index is up 10 percent at the measuring point, you would realize a gain of whatever your cap is (say, 3.5 percent) while the insurer keeps the rest.

If using a "spread" method to limit an annuitant's share of an index gain, the insurance company retains the first X percent of any gain— typically the first 2 to 5 percent—and the investor gets credit for anything above that. Example: your index rises 6 percent in an anniversary year. The insurance company keeps the first, say, 3 percent; you are credited for the remainder.

In a "participation" method, the investor receives credited interest at a designed participation rate of whatever the index gain might be—say, 50 percent of a 10 percent index gain.

An annuity investor often has options on whether his share in any index growth is limited by a cap, spread, or participation rate. The insurance company reserves the right to adjust the cap, spread, or participation rate on an annual basis, and such adjustments can affect the account value growth an annuitant might realize.

TAKING INCOME FROM ANNUITIES: HOP ABOARD THE INCOME RIDER

Taking income from an annuity can be a simple or more detailed process.

In its most basic form, an annuity has an account value that starts as the premium contract value. That value can grow by a fixed amount of interest (in a fixed annuity); it can rise or fall based on the daily performance of the market (in a variable annuity); or it can be linked to the performance of a specific market index with a limit on participation in market growth but protection against market loss (in a fixed index annuity). Without the addition of optional income riders (which we'll discuss in this section), that fluctuating account value represents the future income an annuitant can expect when withdrawals are taken from the contract.

Many people take systematic withdrawals—typically 4 to 5 percent annually—based on the account value. That account value will decrease as withdrawals are made, but one's hope is to at least partially offset that decline with account growth that either matches or comes close to the amount being withdrawn. This is the goal in making a traditional annuity last for a long time.

A note of caution is necessary here before advancing this discussion.

Money invested in an annuity should not be considered liquid. In order to encourage investors to leave their money in their annuity contracts, insurance companies create "surrender periods" to protect the premium payments they invest in the hope of realizing further growth. The typical surrender period for many annuities today is ten years, though they can be longer or shorter.

During this surrender period, an annuity is not a demand deposit account like a savings or checking account. During this period, most annuities allow you to withdraw a percentage of the account value penalty free; 7 to 10 percent is typical. If you withdraw more money from the annuity than the contract allows during the surrender period, you will pay a penalty and may not be able to receive your entire investment amount back. This is because the insurance company has your premium tied up in bonds, Treasuries and other investments with the understanding that they will have this money for a certain period of time. Because they will take a hit when removing money from these investments prematurely, you consequently will pay a surrender charge to make up for their loss. The longer an insurance company can hold your money, the easier it is for them to guarantee a predictable return on it.

Once the surrender period has expired, you can remove your money whenever you want. Your money becomes liquid again because the insurance company has used it in an investment that fits the timeline of your surrender period. For many people, this is an attractive trade off that can provide a creative solution for filling their retirement income gap.

Now let's examine an alternative way to take income from an annuity. Behold, the income rider.

An income rider is a subset of an annuity. Essentially, it is the amount of money upon which the insurance company will base your regular income payments while you have your money in their annuity. Your income rider is often a larger number than the principal you invested and is likely to be greater than your account value.

To illustrate how this works, let's consider a variable or fixed index annuity with an income rider, an add-on option that comes with an additional annual fee of about 1 percent of the account value.

The income rider essentially creates two sides of an annuity contract. One is the account value/cash side of the ledger. This side performs as described above and is typically linked to the performance of the market. This is actual cash you can access, either all at once (presumably outside of the surrender period) or through systematic withdrawals.

The "income side" of the ledger is *not* cash. You can't surrender the policy and receive the income value as you can with the cash value. Nor is the income value affected by the performance of the market. Rather, the income side is a figure that grows by a designated, guaranteed percentage each year—6 to 7 percent a year in many 2019 contracts. This growth is guaranteed by the insurance company based on its confidence in its investment portfolio, which explains why the income value generally exceeds account/cash value in most annuities with income riders.

The income side represents a baseline figure from which the insurance company will determine the size of your regular income payments once you choose to begin receiving them, based on the specifics of the contract. In other words, the regular income you receive from an annuity with an income rider will be based on the income value as opposed to the account/cash value. Moreover, the insurance company is contractually required to make regular payments based on this income figure for as long as the contract is in effect, even if the account/cash value falls to $0. This can be quite attractive as it can create a dependable stream of income for life, similar to a pension.

Some things to note here.

Your account/cash value will diminish with each withdrawal taken, but the income value that is used to determine the amount of each income payment remains frozen at the level it held when payments began.

In other words, if a $200,000 annuity with an income rider sees its income value grow to $282,000 after four years of guaranteed 7 percent growth (minus the fee for the rider), if the income rider is activated, the insurance company might pay 5 percent of that figure annually ($14,000) for as long as the annuitant lives. It will pay that amount based on the $282,000 income value that is frozen when the income rider is activated. The contract's account/cash value will decline when withdrawals begin, but income payments will continue even if that account value falls to $0. (This kind of complete decline is unlikely, however, given that the account value retains its potential to experience offsetting growth due to market gains even after income withdrawals begin.)

One final note. Designated beneficiaries in an annuity contract can receive only the account value, as opposed to the income value, of a contract upon the death of the annuitant. However, a contract that covers spouses allows a surviving spouse to receive continuing income payments based on the income value.

FINAL THOUGHTS ON ANNUITIES

I often get questions from clients about annuities and whether or not they are a good idea. To be perfectly honest, I have no idea if they are a good idea for you, and I can't form an opinion without knowing more about you and your specific situation and goals.

Here's the bottom line. Annuities are popular and reliable tools that allow you to secure sustainable income during retirement, and they may or may not be a good fit for your retirement plan. They can be one of the most efficient ways to generate a guaranteed stream of income during retirement. And while I've said this before, it bears repeating here: Establishing sustainable income streams are one of the best ways to fill income gaps and thus achieve your retirement goals.

Annuities are one way, though hardly the only way, to fill the gap between what you expect to have in retirement expenses and what you expect to receive in sustainable retirement income.

Don't overlook the other income-producing investment tools we discussed back in Chapter Two. You may recall the discussion about investment tools such as CDs, U.S. Treasury bonds, municipal and corporate bonds that produce interest income as well as offer some degree of protection against loss of invested principal.

CHAPTER SEVEN

Accumulation and the Effects of Volatility

Once you have worked with a financial professional to address how you will fund all your regular living expenses, it's now time to take a look at the future. With your immediate income needs met, you have the opportunity to take any additional assets and leverage them for profit to supplement your income in the future.

The assets we're considering here are what we called in an earlier chapter "growth" money as opposed to "lifestyle" money. These are assets you should not count on to meet recurring expenses such as paying the electric bill, buying groceries, or paying your auto insurance.

Rather, these are assets we defined as "red money" back in Chapter Two. By way of review, the defining characteristic of red money is growth potential. These are investments that will see the majority of their return derived from growth in the market. They are different from green and yellow money assets that grow mainly through the generation of interest and dividends. These are assets you hope to grow to use for future needs such as health care or nursing costs, contributions to your legacy plan, or merely taking that dream vacation you've talked about for years.

Basically, the accumulation part of a retirement portfolio is our ace in the hole. Those are the assets we don't want to convert into income until we choose to do so. The goal in managing red-money assets should always be to choose the time and place when it is best for us to turn these assets into income.

It goes without saying, however, that talking about being a good investor—that is, following the age-old advice to sell assets only when the market is high—is considerably easier said than done. People who are nervous about their investments often have a very hard time making good decisions about those investments. The decision-making process becomes emotional, and you don't want to be scared with your red money.

You can be watchful, yes; you certainly don't want to see your red money decline by 40 percent. Yet even in 2008, as bad as that time was for the market, had you been able to hold onto your investments from 2008 through 2018, you'd be in pretty good shape at the end of that time period.

That sounds easy enough, but, in reality, it's actually very difficult and sometimes impossible. We are all human and have worked hard for the money we've saved. Watching the value of our investments decline is both disheartening and scary. Emotions can run high and force us into making bad decisions.

There are also many people in retirement who may not have the luxury of holding all of their investments through a prolonged market downturn simply because they need to sell holdings to pay bills and support their lifestyle. The effects of market volatility can certainly be a difficult beast to tame.

Here is where we go back to the idea of having a solid foundation of yellow and green money that provides retirement income without having to sell shares of the red-money assets. This approach is still the best way I know—especially for people in retirement—to become the kind of investor we've always been taught to be.

DEALING WITH VOLATILITY IN RETIREMENT

Again, this is sometimes easier said than done as a volatile market can raise the eyebrows of even the most veteran investor. Taking a hit during a market downturn, however temporary, hurts no matter how stable your income. Part of the pain comes from knowing that, when you take a step back in the market, it requires an even larger step forward to return to where you once were.

The stress of dealing with major market fluctuations will probably never go away completely, but things can be less stressful to handle if we have a strategy of using income-producing green and yellow money assets to get through the hard times when red, at-risk assets are under attack.

Red money should be like the cherry on top of the sundae. It is our potential for growth, not our principle source of income. When there is inevitable market volatility, the dizzying ups and downs should not matter as much if we're not dependent on this at-risk money for income. When you have steady, reliable streams of green and yellow money meeting your regular living expenses, you may be more comfortable with taking a long-view approach to your red growth money.

A good foundation of green and yellow money allows you to be a better red money investor because you don't have to continually tinker with your portfolio. You are no longer chasing returns because you've already built a plan using other parts of your portfolio to satisfy your income goals and needs. You don't have to sweat the small stuff every day and can better resist emotional, often costly decisions during volatile market times. You can continue in retirement to be the kind of steady investor you worked to be during your working years.

When the market corrects itself and experiences a sharp drop, people often say, "Don't worry, the market will come back," and I agree with that—especially if you've invested in solid companies with consistent earnings and have confidence in the overall American economy. The trouble is, if you've sold shares when the market is down, you now own fewer shares that will experience growth when market prices rebound. Owning fewer shares is never better than having more shares if your goal is to get back to where you were before you made a panic decision to sell at a lower price during a downturn.

My philosophy, as I indicated earlier, is to put clients in a position where they don't have to sell shares unless they want to do so. That option is best realized when you have assets producing dividends and interest that can support your goals and income needs, leaving you in a position where you won't have to sell shares to generate the cash you need.

RED MONEY NEEDS CAUTION, BUT NOT NECESSARILY TIMIDITY

I hope I haven't given anyone the wrong impression with these words of caution. I may be a cautious person, but I'm far from being timid or fearful of participation in the stock market, even in retirement.

An advisor sometimes might be characterized as too conservative, especially if they look too much at the downside of things.

I try to be a little different. I actually love red money. I think it can be an important part of a plan if it fits with a client's goals and needs. But I like red money best when we can invest it in the way it was meant to be invested. That is, when it is used for growth, not to support our daily expenses and income needs.

When you've empowered yourself to invest for the long term, red money can be a wonderful tool. I like the stock market and I worry sometimes that too many advisors are becoming "insurance heavy." All they want to talk about is, "We're going to see 2008 all over again soon." It's not that they're wrong. But I want my clients to be able to say, "so what?" I want them to have the solid income planning to be able to wait the ten or more years it may take for the market to come back. If their lifestyle needs are met for the foreseeable future, their red money can stay invested and maybe come out on top after a big market correction.

The point I'm making here is that get-rich-quick strategies are not very effective over the long run. I prefer retirees use the old-fashioned way; that is, to build wealth and generate income from interest and dividends, to realize growth where we can, and to make sure we're investing for growth over a long-term horizon.

Again, there is nothing new about this concept. It's actually a very old approach, but it's not sexy anymore. But who needs sexy when you're retired? Dependable is much more important.

This whole approach to creating wealth through income generation fell out of fashion for a couple reasons. One, people became greedy as they saw the market going up and up. Two, they also—in part because the financial services industry pushed it this way—got more into mutual fund investing. Rather than do the research necessary to buy individual stocks and other investments, people became convinced instead to buy mutual funds where that research was being done by professional managers.

Well, mutual funds can be suitable for many investors. My approach, however, puts a greater emphasis on choosing individual stocks and investments, ones that pay dividends in addition to their growth potential. Mutual funds are fine for growth, but they don't do much to generate income. That's why when I talk to clients about investment tools—which I do only after determining what their retirement goals and needs are—

I'm more inclined to talk about options we discussed earlier such as preferred stock, corporate bonds, REITs, BDCs, or even dividend-producing common stock.

I believe that, if you're going to have red-money investments, it makes sense to have a portion of the return on that money derived from dividends. It just makes sense to allow a company to pay you to hold their stock. That's what a dividend is.

Keep in mind that you have the option to take those dividends either as income or to reinvest them for future growth. That decision depends on a client's individual needs. I would love to reinvest all dividends, but if a client's goals dictate that they need income, then you take the dividends for that purpose.

The beautiful thing about this concept is that if you have to take your dividends as income, you're not having to sell shares of your red-money assets to generate that income. The dividends are the income. You can better maintain your share amount, which means that during times of market growth your portfolio has the potential to grow in value even as you're getting paid to hold the stock. The dividend itself also has the potential to grow over time if you invest in good companies with a history of increasing dividends.

FINAL THOUGHTS ON RED MONEY AND VOLATILITY

One of the most complete analysis I've seen of market volatility and its effect on human behavior was a 2013 report from DALBAR, the well-respected financial services market research firm. The group's annual "Quantitative Analysis of Investment Behavior" report (QAIB) studied the impact of market volatility on individual investors who manage (or mismanage) their own investments in the stock market.

According to the study, volatility not only caused investors to make decisions based on their emotions, but those decisions also harmed their investments and prevented them from realizing potential gains.

So why do people meddle so much with their investments when the market is fluctuating?

Part of the reason is that many people have financial obligations that they don't have control over. Sudden unexpected expenses such as making a home repair, or repairing or replacing a broken-down car, or paying an emergency medical bill can put people in a position where they need money that is not a part of their regular budget. If they need to sell investments to come up with that money immediately, they don't have the luxury of selling when they want to. They must sell when they need to.

DALBAR's "Quantitative Analysis of Investor Behavior" has been used to measure the effects of investors' buying, selling, and mutual fund switching decisions since 1994. The QAIB shows time and time again that over a nearly twenty-year period the average investor earns less, in many cases significantly less, than the performance of mutual funds suggests.

An excerpt from the report claims that:

"No matter what the state of the mutual fund industry, boom or bust, investment results are more dependent on investor behavior than on fund performance," the report found. "Mutual fund investors who hold on to their investments are more successful than those who time the market."[11]

It doesn't take a financial services market research report to tell you that market volatility is out of your control.

The report demonstrates, however, that before you experience market volatility, you should have an investment plan. Moreover, when the market is fluctuating you should stand by your plan. You should also review and discuss your plan with your financial professional on a regular basis, ensuring he/she is aware of any changes in your goals, financial circumstances, your health, or your risk tolerance.

When the economy is under stress and the markets are volatile, investors can feel vulnerable. That vulnerability causes people to tinker with their portfolios in an attempt to outsmart the market. Good financial professionals, however, don't try to time the market for their clients. They instead try to tap into the gains that can be realized by committing to long-term investment strategies.

They also know that clients with steady, sustained sources of income that are not dependent on at-risk money have a better chance of achieving long-term investment goals.

---

[11] 2013 QAIB, Dalbar, March 2013. https://www.dalbar.com/QAIB

CHAPTER EIGHT

New Ideas for Investing

I see it frequently in my practice; far too often, in my opinion. A new client or a couple comes into my office for a first meeting and tells me about their investment portfolio: 80 to 90 percent mutual funds.

I'm truly happy they had the insight to invest in their future. But after some discussion we get into deeper issues, one of which is:

Why are you still so heavily invested in mutual funds?

I already know a large part of the answer. The mutual funds option was likely recommended by another financial advisor, probably one they liked and trusted. Don't get me wrong; I'm glad they had a good relationship, and I'm not saying they got bad advice. Mutual funds can be a perfectly good way to begin investing, especially for younger savers who are just starting out. Mutual funds are an investment tool the financial services industry has pushed for years.

But, it's a lazy way to invest, in my opinion, for people approaching or into retirement.

I say this because I believe there are better options available today for retirement-aged investors who 1) need income, 2) want some kind of principal protection while 3) still realizing some potential for growth in their invested money.

Don't get me wrong, mutual funds may be a great strategy for a given retirement plan, but not because they were used to grow the assets in a 401(k) throughout our working years. Let me explain.

Mutual funds are generally growth vehicles. During our working years, most people have a basic set of financial goals that may include supporting their family, helping their children with educational expenses and growing their savings so they can attain their ultimate goal that is retirement. Mutual funds are very possibly one of the better options available.

79

However, when you get close to retirement, I think it's probably safe to assume that most people have changed their financial goals. The kids have probably graduated from school and started their adult lives, lifestyles have changed considerably, and many people are much more concerned with keeping their nest egg intact and replacing their income stream as opposed to taking more risk to aggressively grow their assets.

Assuming this sounds familiar, I would encourage you to ask yourself a question. If your financial goals have changed, do you think it makes sense to consider a new investment strategy to achieve your new goals? I certainly do, and I would encourage you to spend a little time thinking about it.

Let me introduce three terms here—words with which you are no doubt familiar—to describe what many retirees seek in a retirement plan: liquidity, safety, return.

Mutual funds certainly provide the potential for return, another way of describing growth in an investment. They also provide some degree of liquidity; that is, the ability to create income through the sale of fund shares. What they lack, however, is any degree of safety. Market volatility means you might realize a profit or take a loss when you sell shares to create income, something we discussed in the previous chapter.

The sad fact is that you can't really have all three factors—liquidity, safety, return—in any one product. You can maximize two of the three, but you do so at the expense of the third. Getting all three would be part of the perfect investment, and I've yet to see one of those.

The idea of three dimensions in any investment is a relatively new concept in the financial services industry. Allow me to explain that.

One of the most traditional ways of thinking about investing is the risk-versus-reward trade-off. It goes something like this.

Products that are considered "safer" carry less risk, but also offer the potential for less return. Riskier options carry the burden of volatility and a greater potential for loss, but they also offer a greater potential for rewards. Most professionals move their clients back and forth along this 2-D range, shifting between products that are relatively safer and products that are structured for growth. Essentially, the old rules of investing dictate you can either choose relative safety or return, but you can't have both.

Updated strategies work with the flexibility of a third dimension—liquidity—to remake the rules.

Adding the concept of liquidity to the equation gives an investor the opportunity to maximize any two of our investment dimensions. The chance to realize two dimensions is better than one, but hoping to get all three is asking for too much.

Choosing safety and liquidity is like keeping your assets in a checking or savings account. Bank accounts provide a lot of safety and liquidity but do so at the expense of any return. In today's still low interest rate environment, you are simply not going to see much return generated by money sitting in the bank.

On the other hand, you can opt for an investment offering liquidity and return. This gives you the potential for greater growth, even as you retain the ability to reclaim your money whenever you choose, such as in selling shares of common stock or mutual funds. But, as is the case with selling any equity or commodity, you will likely be exposed to a higher level of risk and volatility.

Understanding liquidity can help you break the old risk-versus-safety trade-off. By identifying which assets you can afford to have less liquid, you can commit them to investments that have higher long-term return to meet your needs and goals while limiting unnecessary risk.

Choosing safety and return over liquidity can have significant impacts on the accumulation of your assets. Let's look at that more closely in this hypothetical example involving Ted, whose retirement-related paradigm shift from earning and saving to leveraging assets was a costly one.

TED IS LOSING MONEY SAFELY

Ted is a corn and soybean farmer with a small livestock operation. He owns 1,200 acres of land. He routinely keeps somewhere between $40,000 and $80,000 in his checking and savings accounts in case a major piece of equipment needs repair or replacement. This way, Ted has readily available emergency money to pay for the equipment so he can carry on with farming.

Ted deals routinely with rising and falling commodity prices, as all farmers do. If the price of feed for his cattle goes up one year, he will need to compensate for the increased overhead. The same adjustment is necessary when prices fall on the grain he sells, and his revenue is decreased. And like all farmers, Ted always lives with the uncertainty of weather's effect on his crops.

Bottom line, Ted knows how to manage his business by making necessary adjustments. Even so ...

Ted isn't a particularly wealthy farmer, so he has little choice but to keep a portion of his money close at hand in case something comes up and he must access it quickly. Most of his capital is held in livestock in the pasture or crops in the ground, meaning this money is tied up for six to eight months of the year. When a major financial need arises, Ted can't just harvest ten additional acres of soybeans and use that additional revenue for payment. He needs to depend heavily on liquidity in order to be a successful farmer.

In time, Ted decides he's had enough of the grind of daily farming. Old habits die hard, however, and even after Ted sells the farm and his equipment, he still keeps his bank accounts flush with cash, just like in the old days. Ted keeps a huge portion of the profits from the sale of land and machinery in liquid investments because that's what he's always done.

Unfortunately for Ted, that pile of money sitting in his bank account isn't keeping pace with inflation. After all his hard work as a farmer, his money is losing value every day because he didn't leverage his assets to generate income and accumulate value.

Ted, in short, is losing money safely, never a good idea. But that's what happens when your money devalues through inflation. If you keep your money in a savings account or a bank CD paying 1 percent—lower than the rate of inflation—you are essentially losing money in the safest place you can keep it.

Ted's money was as liquid as it could be, but almost anything would have been a better option. Even as cautious as he is, Ted might have pursued some relatively conservative options with the potential to outperform inflation if only he'd been willing to think outside the box.

By sacrificing some liquidity, for example, Ted might have realized relative safety and return through the purchase of corporate bonds. Though no bond is 100 percent safe—they don't have FDIC protection like the money in Ted's bank accounts—corporate bonds issued by America's most reputable companies rarely default. Moreover, they pay a fixed rate of return (interest) as long as you hold them. You lose some liquidity if you hold that bond to maturity, but such is the trade-off for a far better inflation-beating return than Ted is getting from his bank. Again, you can have any two of the investment dimensions, but not all three.

Or, Ted might have considered combining liquidity and return/growth with the purchase of dividend-producing preferred stock. Liquidity is available here in that you can sell shares anytime you need income, but the trade-off is in safety due to the volatility of the market. You can gain or lose value in the exchange of any stock, either preferred or common.

One more option Ted might have pursued was the relative safety and return through investing in an equity index annuity that offers protection against loss of principal due to market volatility. This annuity also offers the potential for interest-credited growth in a market index. The sacrifice, again, is liquidity, as an annuity is a long-term contract.

As Ted's tale illustrates, choosing liquidity alone can be a costly option. The sooner you want your money back, the less you can leverage it for safety or return. On the other hand, if you put your money in a long-term investment, you sacrifice liquidity for the chance to realize a greater return. Rethinking your approach to money in this way can make a world of difference in providing you with a structured way to generate income while allowing the value of your assets to grow over time.

TAKE A NEW LOOK AT YOUR RETIREMENT PORTFOLIO

Restructuring your investment portfolio in the years prior to or early in retirement just makes sense to me. After all, your life is about to change. Your ability to generate income is about to change. Your goals and your needs also are likely to change.

Your goals were likely very different when you were working and raising a family. You worked then to pay your mortgage or rent as well as to provide both essential and non-essential comforts for your children, your spouse, and yourself. Anything left in your paycheck after addressing family needs was put away for retirement, or so we hope. Your investment strategy then was for growth with an eye on the future, and the tools you used then were growth tools. You likely used mutual funds, which can be good growth tools for people without a great deal of investing expertise.

But as you transition into retirement, your goals and needs change.

The kids are grown now with children of their own. Your mortgage is either paid off or close to being so. You no longer have regular wages, but you also are no longer tied to a desk or other work commitment. Your new goals now may include travel, hobbies, or spending more time with friends or grandkids. Maybe you want to make charitable contributions or provide future money for your loved ones. And, yes, you still have financial obligations to meet, and you are probably more concerned now than ever before about how to fund future health care needs.

When your goals change, your investment strategies also should probably change. In retirement you will find yourself needing more than just a growth strategy. You will also need an income strategy, an investment strategy, a tax strategy, and an estate strategy.

Goal-based planning—an approach I strongly advocate—can be especially important when your goals change as you enter this life phase.

Goal planning differs from the traditional application of "retirement formulas" you hear from many financial companies or their representatives. These formulas are part of the conventional wisdom approach that says one key to a successful retirement is to have income that is X percentage of whatever you made in the everyday work force.

I'm not a big fan of overly simplistic retirement formulas. I just don't find that using a formula based on what your salary was in your working years is particularly useful in retirement. Such a formula may, in fact, be totally useless for some people.

This is because the factors in the retirement equation are often totally different from what you knew earlier in life when you were more concerned with, say, financing a college education for your kids. In retirement, however, your concerns should be more about you. Sure, you still think about providing for a spouse and leaving something for the kids. But you are also allowed—or should I say, encouraged—to think about doing some fun things you've always wanted to do, in addition to addressing less-entertaining issues such as health care.

A goals-planning approach first takes into consideration what you want from life in retirement, then sets out to explore the financial tools and means to make those goals financially feasible.

To be sure, sometimes overly ambitious retirement goals and dreams must be scaled down somewhat when the numbers don't add up. But in other instances, clients are sometimes pleasantly surprised to learn they can do more in retirement than they thought possible. I'm pleased to report I often deal with the second circumstance more than the first.

Let's take a look at how we might restructure a retirement portfolio using a goal-oriented approach. Addressing liquidity, safety, and growth in this restructuring is an essential part of the process.

THE LIQUIDITY FACTOR

The first question is, how much liquidity do you really need? There is no way to fully address this question without first having done some basic expense-vs-income calculations, which as we discussed earlier is the first step in drawing up a retirement income plan.

If you haven't sat down and created an income plan for your retirement, your perceived need for liquidity is just a guess. For one thing, you don't know how much cash you'll need to fill the income gap if you don't know the amount of your Social Security benefit or the total of your other income options. For another, you won't be able to make an even educated guess about how much you might need for a short-term emergency such as a major household or auto repair, dealing with a natural disaster or needing cash to pay your share of what insurance or Medicare doesn't cover on a major surgery.

But once you have determined your income need and have a plan to fill those needs, then you can partition your assets based on when you will need them. With an income plan in place, you can use new rules to pursue both safety and return from your assets.

So, back to our first question: How much of your money might you want in cash or reasonably liquid assets? We don't need an exact figure, but a percentage of the total retirement portfolio should be set aside to address situations that might require some immediate and significant cash.

If a client wants quick access to, say, 5 percent of a hypothetical portfolio we'll value at $600,000, that means $30,000 will be earmarked for cash.

There are different options we can use to keep that cash close at hand. Savings and checking accounts are the most liquid, but have the lowest return. A CD or even "laddered CDs"—deposits made at different times and for different durations to give us a greater degree of interest and liquidity—can give us less liquidity but with slightly higher interest. . Or, for more income potential, U.S. Treasury's or a fixed annuity may tie up at least part of your money for a longer period of time but will return a higher rate of interest.

THE SAFETY FACTOR

Next, let's look at the element of safety.

This is somewhat comparable to setting the foundation and building the frame of a new house before the finishing work can begin. Here is where we determine how much of a portfolio the client wants protected from loss of invested principal due to market volatility—the financial industry's legal description of what most investors simply call "safety."

Again, the answer varies depending on the risk tolerance of individual clients. Some might want half of their retirement money protected from loss of principal due to market fluctuations. Some will want more than that, others less.

Let's say the mythical client we described before wants 50 percent of a portfolio "protected." We've already earmarked 5 percent ($30,000) of his $600,000 for liquidity, so we have 45 percent ($270,000) to be protected.

Here is where we might discuss any number of investment options that offer principal protection. There also are several options to consider that offer various levels of growth potential and liquidity.

We now have allocated 50 percent of the portfolio to a division of cash and other assets that have the potential to grow and produce income without risk of market-performance loss. Now we have the opportunity to look to the future.

THE TOTAL RETURN FACTOR

Half of our portfolio remains to be allocated. Our mythical client's risk tolerance as he or she prepares for retirement is somewhere between "I don't want to lose any money" and "Let it all ride on red." In other words, he or she is willing to take some risk with assets they don't need for immediate income in the hope of realizing a greater long-term reward.

Here is where I like to present investment options that produce income through dividends and interest while also having some potential for market-related growth.

Here is where we might talk about investing the remaining $300,000 of the portfolio in some combination of non-guaranteed assets. We might talk about a combination of corporate bonds, preferred stock, real estate, business development trusts, limited liability corporations or even common stock in companies with a solid history of earnings. Again, our eye here is on investments that will grow in value through dividends and interest as opposed to strictly through daily rises and falls in market value.

Presto, your retirement portfolio has been restructured using investment tools that address your specific wishes regarding liquidity, safety, and return/growth.

PLAN FOR WHAT YOU EXPECT AS WELL AS THE UNEXPECTED
The mythical portfolio we just described brings us back full circle to a concept we discussed in Chapter Two, "The Color of Money." We talked then about the importance in retirement planning of filling three distinct buckets with:

1) Conservative, readily accessible cash (green money).

2) Assets that produce reliable income while offering some degree of relative safety along with some potential for limited growth (yellow money).

3) Assets invested for long-term growth with risk-reward exposure to market volatility (red money).

Check out the above portfolio and you will recognize each of these money buckets being addressed.

How we go about filling those buckets remains a highly individualized choice, one that should be based on a person's goals and needs as opposed to a financial representative's recommendation. My belief is that it is only after clients outline their retirement goals and dreams can an advisor explore appropriate financial tools and options. Too often, I'm sorry to say, I see examples of the planning process beginning with discussions of products and investments. This makes achieving your financial goals a bit of a gamble.

Look at it this way. Anyone who has ever planned a vacation knows you first have to know where you want to go and what you want to do upon arriving before you start talking about how you get there or whether you can afford it.

People on the cusp of retirement need to take time to think about what it is they want or expect in this new phase of life. They should think about the things they'd like to do—more travel, more relaxation, more recreation, more time with friends and family. These goals should be the basis of any retirement plan, the foundation upon which a financial advisor can restructure assets amassed during the working years into a plan that will fill all three money buckets in retirement.

But we also must prepare for the unexpected.

"Life" just happens sometimes. These are the unavoidable things we don't look forward to, and increasing health care needs are at the top of that list. We don't know where or when "life" will happen, or what the cards will look like when they're dealt. We can, however, build a plan that gives us options to play whatever cards we're dealt as well as we can.

This plan, as I've repeated often in this book, will have a strong base of income-producing assets that will fill the income gap without a large exposure to market fluctuations. Having done that, such a plan also allows a retirement investor to take whatever level of risk is desired with market-exposed growth assets.

One other important point I thinks bears repeating here.

Among the goals of such a plan is removing the emotion often associated with investing in general, and retirement investing in particular.

In retirement, you don't want to be affected by the day-to-day volatility of the market. You want to know you have reliable income that will be there regardless of market performance. You want to know you don't have to sell market-exposed assets to generate essential income.

You also want to know you are working with a financial advisor capable of putting together a well-managed investment account that meets your goals as a whole, not in individualized and piecemeal ways.

Professional money managers do this by creating requirements for each type of investment in which they put your money.

Every investor has a different goal, and every goal requires a customized strategy. A professional will create a portfolio that reflects your investment desires. If some of the current assets you own complement the strategies that your professional recommends, those will likely stay in your portfolio.

Does some of this sound familiar? It should.

Many of these "new ideas" for investing are actually age-old concepts that have somehow been forgotten or set aside in favor of so-called new-age strategies. But I happen to believe that some old-school ideas—finding what a client wants and needs, finding the right tool for the right job, acting in a client's best interest—worked well in the past and will continue to work well today.

CHAPTER NINE

Taxes and Retirement

Throughout your many years in the workforce, you no doubt were advised frequently about the value of investing in tax-deferred retirement savings plans. The conventional wisdom about such plans went something like this:

Workers with the foresight to participate in retirement plans such as 401(k)s, IRAs, self-employment plans (SEPs), 403(b)s, and other options invested in their future via pre-tax withholding payments taken from their paychecks. These tax-deferred contributions lowered your taxable income during your wage-earning years and delayed the taxes you owed on those wages until, in theory, you were in a lower tax bracket in retirement.

No doubt, tax-deferred retirement savings plans are a wonderful tool used by millions of workers who look forward to the time they no longer have to be part of the daily work grind. I applaud my clients who were able to use such plans to their advantage.

Even so, there are a couple of things people are not told when investing for their future, yet, these are things they need to know in the years approaching retirement as will soon become abundantly clear.

1. Yes, many people earn less income and do fall into a lower tax bracket in retirement. But that's not always the case. Many other people in retirement have goals of generating income that comes close, if not fully matches, the income they received in the workforce. Depending on how they structured their retirement savings, such people could well find themselves in the same tax bracket they knew previously in life.

2. Taxes in retirement can be more complex than those we routinely deal with in our working years. For example: Income you take from tax-deferred accounts can have consequences that produce something of a double whammy on your overall tax picture. Not only is your regular

taxable income increased—possibly to the point that you might be elevated into a higher tax bracket—but this additional income also could increase the amount of tax you might pay on your Social Security benefits. Moreover, there will come a time in retirement when you (or a surviving spouse or other heirs) will be required to take taxable distributions from tax-deferred accounts.

In short, the savings we've accumulated over the years that have benefitted from tax deferral may not be all we thought they would be when we enter retirement. We may not find ourselves in an effectively lower tax bracket then. This is primarily a reflection of the reduced deductions available in retirement. We will explore much of this in more detail throughout the next two chapters.

TAX PLANNING VS. MERE TAX REPORTING

Taxes in retirement are often considered a debt obligation that ranks No. 2 (behind only health care costs) among the drains on a retirement nest egg. Taxes add another component to the retirement equation, one that says it matters less how much you've saved for retirement as does how much you get to keep. I tend to agree with the philosophy that says a person can increase earning power more in retirement by limiting taxes than in making more money.

Retirement then is a time when it becomes more important than ever to do real tax planning as opposed to mere tax reporting.

Tax planning and tax reporting are two very different things. Most people only report their taxes. March rolls around and they gather up their W-2 and 1099 statements and set about filing out their annual 1040 report. They enter their income numbers and then work to get every possible deduction. At the end of an often-maddening process they either a) curse the bottom line and write a check to the IRS, or b) smile and ship off the completed return, counting the days until the arrival of a refund check.

True tax planning, on the other hand, gives one the option of being proactive with your taxes and planning for the future by making smart, informed decisions about how taxes affect the overall financial plan. Tax planning means working with a financial professional who, along with a CPA, makes recommendations about tax strategies that will help you look forward, as opposed to checking the rearview mirror as you prepare to pay taxes in retirement.

The first step in tax planning is understanding how some things will be different in retirement from what you knew in your workforce years.

The main reason for the difference is the obvious change in lifestyle and earnings from your workings years. This is the essential difference between the "accumulation phase" of your working years and the "distribution phase" you begin upon entering retirement.

While we were working, we had a job and collected a paycheck that withheld through payroll deductions some—sometimes more, sometimes less—of our tax obligation. People who have taxes withheld on a regular basis often tend not to think about this money they haven't seen until they are forced to consider it every year as April 15 approaches. Our working years also are a time of other tax deductions. We may have had a mortgage and gotten a tax deduction on the mortgage interest. We likely had children and the deduction that goes for dependents.

But when we retire, our tax picture takes on a different look. Many people no longer have tax withholding taken from their regular income streams such as Social Security, distributions from tax-deferred accounts or pension or annuity payments. They tend to pay their tax bill in one large, often intimidating check once a year, or in quarterly estimated payments. People tend to think a lot about tax payments when big chunks of their money go out the door all at once.

Many people also make a goal of having their mortgage paid off before or shortly after entering retirement. It's a wonderful goal but it creates a bit of a tax challenge when that mortgage interest deduction goes away. It's also most likely that by the time a couple retires, their children have long since grown up and moved out, thereby eliminating a deduction for dependents. (And even if they move back in, heaven help you, they are adults now and can no longer be counted as dependents.)

The point is, some deductions we once counted on are drastically reduced in retirement. That can majorly affect the overall tax picture.

Something else goes away in retirement. The money we routinely contributed to tax-deferred IRAs and 401(k)s either stops or is greatly limited. Not only is our ability to reduce taxable income decreased, we also increase taxable income with distributions taken from these tax-deferred accounts. These distributions that are fully taxed as ordinary income can become especially problematic when we are required to take them—whether we need them or not—beginning at age seventy-two. We'll discuss Required Minimum Distributions in more detail later in this chapter.

That's problem No. 1.

Problem No. 2 is that our tax system is set up in a way that the withdrawal of tax-deferred money can have a lever effect on other components of your tax structure. This is especially true when it comes to Social Security.

TAXES ON SOCIAL SECURITY

It comes as a surprise to many people to learn their Social Security benefits might be taxed. Hey, they will say indignantly, didn't I have Social Security taxes withheld from my paycheck ever since the first time I earned one?

You did indeed, and that was your contribution to the Social Security Trust Fund that 1) helped pay benefits to retired workers already receiving them, and 2) were invested by Uncle Sam to make benefits available to future generations.

Social Security benefits were not always taxed and are still not taxed today for people who fall below a certain income level.

The New Deal-era legislation establishing Social Security was signed into law by President Franklin Roosevelt in 1935, and for its first several decades went untaxed. That tax-free streak was then broken in the 1980s under President Ronald Reagan and changed again in the 1990s under President Bill Clinton.

In 1983, in an effort to bolster the long-term viability of Social Security, a new law set up an income threshold for both single filers and joint filers. Any amount of "provisional income"—which we will define here shortly—that exceeded the threshold amount meant that up to 50 percent of your Social Security benefit could be taxed. Congress doubled down on that strategy in 1993 by adding an additional higher threshold over which up to 85 percent of your benefit could be taxed.

"Provisional income" is a figure that includes all elements of regular adjusted gross income as reported on your annual tax return. Your tax return includes wages earned, pension and annuity payments, ordinary dividends and interest, the taxable part of distributions taken from tax-deferred accounts, self-employment income, capital gains, alimony, rental income, etc. Your provisional income, however, will also include half the amount of Social Security benefits paid to an individual or couple along with any tax-free interest from bonds (most commonly, municipal bonds).

Provisional income determines how much of your Social Security benefits can be subject to taxation.

The first tax on Social Security benefits determined that up to 50 percent of a Social Security benefit could be taxed for single filers with provisional income of more than $25,000, or for a couple filing jointly exceeding $32,000 in provisional income. The second level established that single filers exceeding $34,000 in annual provisional income, and joint filers exceeding $44,000 could have up to 85 percent of benefits subject to taxation at a filer's normal tax rate.

One troubling aspect of these taxation thresholds is they have never been adjusted for inflation. Never! The 85 percent income threshold for a couple filing jointly ($44,000, and $34,000 for a single filer) isn't especially steep by today's inflation-adjusted standards. As a result, it is entirely possible that many more people than expected will now be paying tax on up to 85 percent of their Social Security benefits.

The good news is single filers with less than $25,000 in provisional income, and joint filers with less than $32,000 pay no tax on Social Security benefits.

These thresholds get especially interesting when you consider the effect of withdrawals from tax-deferred accounts. Each dollar taken from a "qualified account"—that is, a tax-deferred account such as an IRA or 401(k)—adds another dollar to your provisional income that in turn determines the tax on your Social Security.

This is the double whammy I referred to earlier. You will pay ordinary income tax on any distribution from a tax-deferred account. That's part of the deal you got when you paid no tax on those IRA or 401(k) contributions during your working years. But now comes an added punch in the form of an IRS rule that requires you to begin taking distributions from tax-deferred accounts whether you want to or not. These required distributions, mind you, also add to provisional income and a possible increase in your Social Security taxes.

Welcome to the world of required minimum distributions (RMDs), a part of the IRS code that makes taxes in retirement very challenging.

REQUIRED MINIMUM DISTRIBUTIONS

As noted, your contributions to qualified, tax-deferred accounts—as well as any growth in those accounts—have never been taxed. But there comes a time when we have to pay the piper.

This is our friendly Uncle Sam, and eventually he will require you to pay tax on your previously tax-deferred investments. That time comes when you reach age seventy-two, the point at which you must begin taking fully taxable required minimum distributions. Again, these RMDs must be taken whether you need the income or not.

The amount of each mandatory distribution is determined by an IRS formula that uses mortality tables to determine a minimum percentage you must take annually from the total value of all your qualified accounts. That percentage starts between 3 and 4 percent at age seventy-two and will increase each year. At age eighty-five, for example, the effective percentage rate for an RMD reaches 6.7 percent.

A note here. One does not have to take a distribution from every qualified account to satisfy RMD obligations. Rather, one has to meet a total number based on the value of all qualified accounts. That total number can be taken from one or any combination of accounts. This can make strategic distributions possible from accounts that fared better due to market performance on a year-to-year basis.

One can, of course, always take more than a required minimum distribution from qualified accounts. But there is a penalty for taking less than the required amount, and that penalty is significant.

If you do not take any required distributions, or if your distributions are not enough, you may have to pay a 50 percent excise tax on the amount not distributed as required.[12] Example: Let's say your RMD number at age

---

[12] "Retirement Topics: Required Minimum Distributions (RMDs)," www.irs.gov

seventy-two is $9,000 but you fail to take any distribution. The IRS penalty is $4,500—half of the $9,000 you should have taken. Now let's say you took a distribution of only $7,000 after a miscalculation of your RMD. The IRS might impose a 50 percent excise tax of $1,000 on the $2,000 you should have taken but didn't. Provisions exist for appeals or waivers of an RMD penalty, but this is one rule you want to be forward-thinking about.

A few more bookkeeping notes here.

Previously, IRS rules were that RMDs began at age seventy-and-one-half, which led to some complicated calendar mathematics surrounding half birthdays and tax deadlines. Since the late-2019 passage of the SECURE Act, however, RMDs begin at age seventy-two, and you must take the required distribution by December 31.[13]

Let's conclude this basic description of RMDs by repeating an important point one final time:

The money you are required to take in distributions, whether you want it or not, has two effects. One, it produces a taxable event on the money you must withdraw, and these distributions are taxed as ordinary income at your regular tax rate. Two, these distributions increase your overall income. This could elevate you into a higher tax bracket as well as increase the chance you might pay additional taxes on Social Security benefits.

If there is any good news here it is this: If you are paying taxes in retirement, it means you have more than bare-bones income. So much for looking on the bright side.

A HELPFUL HINT: KEEP TAX-DEFERRED ACCOUNTS UNDER ONE FINANCIAL UMBRELLA

Dealing with RMDs isn't especially difficult when your tax-deferred accounts are relatively simple. They can be even less of a concern if these accounts are invested in strategies that are focused on efficiently

---

[13] *People whose tax-deferred accounts are still in 401(k)s, profit-sharing plans, 403(b)s and other defined-contribution plan have the potential to realize a different "required beginning date" for RMDs than do people whose tax-deferred plans are in IRAs. Those in defined-contribution plans must take an initial RMD by April 1 of the year following the later of the year you turn seventy-two or the year you retire (if allowed by the plan).* Source: RMD Comparison Chart (IRAs vs. Defined Benefit Plans)." www.irs.gov

generating interest and dividends that can be distributed as part of, or all of, your RMD. This is a powerful concept, and one I encourage you to investigate as it enables you to more effectively make smart investment decisions based upon market conditions and your personal financial goals. Without this type of strategy, you may find yourself selling your investments at inopportune times during years when the market is down simply to generate cash needed for the RMD. This is certainly not a position in which you want to find yourself.

When you have qualified accounts with an RMD obligation, your financial representative, or the company that administers your accounts, is required to annually report that obligation to you. The distribution you are required to take in one calendar year is based on the total value of all qualified accounts from the previous year. Example: the RMD you must take by December 31, 2019, is based on the total value of all qualified accounts on December 31, 2018. You will receive a notice, typically by late January 2019, advising you of the 2018 RMD you must meet.

But things aren't always simple, and sometimes people make costly RMD mistakes.

This might happen because people—often those who manage their own retirement money without professional help—fail to fully understand the requirement. Others might make an incorrect RMD calculation, which is easy to do when dealing with multiple accounts. Couples sometimes have difficulty when both spouses are required to take RMDs and one spouse takes withdrawals from the other's account. People have been known to miss RMDs because of health emergencies and even natural disasters. Fortunately, the IRS has a procedure through which penalties on missed RMDs can be waived, but you have to take the missed deduction and self-report the mistake in a timely manner in addition to providing a reasonable explanation for it.

People who inherit IRAs after the death of the original owner face a particular challenge. Some such people are often too young to be familiar with the RMD concept, or may not know precisely what is required, or when. Yet they too might have to pay a penalty when failing to take RMDs on inherited accounts.

(We'll discuss inherited IRAs in more detail in Chapter Ten.)

One way to reduce the chance of RMD mistakes is to have all your tax-deferred accounts under one financial umbrella—having one quarterback calling the play, so to speak.

Again, every financial company with whom you have qualified accounts has a legal obligation to report your yearly RMD obligation. A problem can arise, however, when you have accounts spread all over the place with different financial representatives. It can sometimes get confusing trying to determine a total RMD number when receiving information from multiple reporting sources.

This is why I believe RMD bookkeeping can be easier when all your qualified accounts are under one umbrella, one financial professional. Not only will you receive your total RMD number from one source, you also will have one person with full knowledge of your investment situation to help you make good decisions on the accounts from which your mandatory distributions are taken.

It's likely not most effective to take your RMD amount from every single qualified account. You may have one account that is outperforming others, making it the prime candidate from which to take all or most of your RMDs. Or, you may have a qualified account with some protection against losses—for instance, a 401(k) that was rolled into an annuity as part of a personal IRA. It may be more advantageous to take an RMD from that account than from one experiencing market volatility.

Here is where working with a professional can be important.

By having a quarterback managing the overall picture, a person has the chance to be more tax efficient and make better decisions on the overall management of their portfolio, overall optimizing their opportunities.

To repeat a point made frequently in this book: If you can generate a reliable stream of income through interest and dividends, you can better avoid situations where you might make bad investment decisions when forced to sell assets to generate income. The same concept applies here in our discussion of RMDs when it comes time to decide from which qualified accounts you want to take withdrawals to meet RMD obligations.

Let's look at this another way. Your financial professional might help you position assets to produce interest and dividends that cover at least some of the taxes you will owe on any RMD liability.

I'm a big believer that the taxes due on RMDs should be paid from sources other than the tax-deferred accounts themselves. Sure, you can always meet your tax obligation by having withholding taken from any distribution, just as was done with your regular paycheck. But paying taxes from proceeds taken from tax-deferred accounts effectively reduces the value of the IRA and defeats much of the purpose of these retirement savings plans.

I believe instead in developing other ways to pay taxes. These could include the use of itemized deductions to offset some of the tax burden, or generating income designed specifically to pay taxes, a retirement expense that will be as inevitable as your regular utility bills and should budgeted for accordingly.

We'll talk in the next chapter about dealing with the tax bill created whenever money is moved out of a tax-deferred account, voluntarily or otherwise. But let's look first at how we might set up a more tax-efficient portfolio that can help accomplish our goal of reducing taxes in retirement.

BUILDING A DIVERSIFIED TAX PORTFOLIO

Building a diversified tax portfolio begins with filling three kinds of investment 'buckets" with an eye on the tax implications of each. Those buckets are:

Taxable. This is money in bank accounts, brokerage accounts or anything else that produces taxable interest, dividends and capital gains. The principal in these accounts—the money you saved in the bank or invested in a brokerage account—has already been taxed, but you will receive 1099 notices each year reporting taxable dividends, interest, and capital gains. This is green, liquid money, not likely to produce a lot of income, but it can prove helpful in managing the overall tax efficiency of your entire portfolio. Money from our taxable bucket—and Social Security benefits are part of this bucket—might be used to pay taxes incurred on withdrawals from tax-deferred accounts.

Tax-deferred. This is the money we described before in qualified retirement accounts such as a 401(k), IRA, 403 (b), or SEP. Money in these accounts has not yet been taxed as it was invested on a pre-tax basis. You pay ordinary income tax on this money only when it is withdrawn, and you now know there is a time when you will be required to make such withdrawals. The ordinary income tax you pay on withdrawals depends on the tax bracket you are in.

Tax-advantaged. The Roth IRA—which we will discuss in greater detail in the next chapter—and municipal bonds are the leading examples of the few options available here. Money invested here is done on an after-tax basis, but its growth within the account is tax-free. Better yet, all withdrawals from the account also are tax-free when done according to the rules governing Roth IRAs.[14] In addition, withdrawals from Roth accounts do not count as provisional income, which as you now know can affect Social Security taxation. Contributions to a Roth IRA are subject to limitations based on income, though Roth conversions—moving money from a traditional IRA or 401(k) into a Roth, a taxable event—are not. (Much more on Roth conversions in Chapter Ten.) Building up a Roth IRA over time can give a person in retirement opportunities to take tax-free withdrawals that can help pay taxes, pay bills, or finance the more enjoyable expenses of retirement.

Having money in all three tax buckets gives a person the opportunity to develop tax strategies that can help control or even reduce tax liability in retirement.

Consider, for instance, how one might deploy assets in different buckets to defray the effects of capital gains taxes imposed on profits realized from the sale of any capital asset such as stock, bonds, commodities, property, or a share of a business, among other things.

An investor with a professionally managed portfolio, also known as actively managed accounts, might consider whether such accounts belong in a taxable or tax-deferred bucket. These accounts likely contain stocks, bonds, ETFs, and other equities that are routinely bought and sold by professional portfolio managers in an attempt to generate the best return they can get for you, the person paying for their services. Each trade has the potential to produce a capital gain that can generate a taxable event.

---

[14] *A qualified distributions from a Roth IRA can be excluded from gross income if a) it occurs at least five years after the first Roth contribution; b) if the account owner has reached age fifty-nine-and-a-half; c) if the account holder is disabled; or d) on or after the account holder's death.* Source: "Designated Roth Accounts: Distributions." www.irs.gov

One way to limit the effects of capital gains—especially if they represent a significant amount of your annual tax burden—is to have your actively managed accounts included in your tax-deferred bucket, perhaps as an investment choice within a personal IRA. In this way, capital gains help grow the value of the account on a tax-deferred basis and the tax on those gains is paid only when money is withdrawn.

On the other hand, capital gains taxes are not a problem for everyone, as not everyone pays them. The Tax Cuts and Jobs Act of 2017 established that single filers with taxable income below $39,375, and joint filers below $78,750 will pay zero tax on capital gains. Single filers with taxable incomes between $39,376 and $434,550, as well as joint filers between $78,751 and $488,850 pay a 15 percent rate on capital gains. Incomes above those limits can see capital gains taxed at a 20 percent rate. This law will "sunset" (expire) in 2025, so it is likely that these details will be different in the future.

Some people in retirement find capital gains taxes are not a major concern. Such people might very comfortably have actively managed accounts as part of their taxable bucket.

Keep in mind, too, that any sale of a capital asset can produce a loss as well as a gain. The effective use of capital losses—which can offset the effects of capital gains and serve as a way of reducing taxable income—is something you might discuss with your financial professional or a CPA with whom they have a business relationship. Both can offer advice on the most tax-efficient way of reporting capital losses.

One more note on capital gains. As they are a component of both taxable income and provisional income, they can become a factor in 1) elevating the taxpayer into a higher income bracket in which capital gains are taxed at a higher rate, and 2) increasing the taxation of Social Security. Clearly, attempting to control or limit capital gains in retirement—giving careful consideration to the timing and selling of capital assets—is a tax strategy worth discussing with your financial professional.

Other tax strategies might include withdrawing money from tax-deferred accounts during tax years when you have a large amount of deductions; sheltering retirement assets from taxation through charitable giving; or moving taxable assets into irrevocable trusts or other tax shelters. Again, we'll look at some of these options in more detail in the next chapter.

IT'S NEVER TOO LATE, OR TOO EARLY, TO START TAX PLANNING

Tax planning can work strongly in your favor during all phases of life. In the distribution phase, however, it can be especially significant. This is when you have a more predictable income based on your pension and Social Security benefits, or money you know you must take in RMDs as well as any other income-generating assets you may have. What impacts you most at this stage is how much of that money you keep in your pocket after taxes.

Essentially, you will make more money in retirement by saving on taxes than you will by making more money. If you can reduce your tax burden by 30, 20 or even 10 percent, you earn that much more money by not paying it in taxes.

How do you save money on taxes? By having a plan. In this instance, a financial professional can work with a CPA either within their firm, or associated with it, to create a distribution plan that can help to minimize your taxes and maximize your annual net income.

The implications of proactive tax planning are farther reaching than many people realize. Remember, doing your taxes in January, February, March or April is mere tax reporting, recapping a story that occurred in the previous tax year. But real tax planning, done well in advance of tax reporting, gives you an opportunity to shape that story as it happens. You can look in advance at all the factors at play and make decisions that will impact your tax return before you file it.

This kind of planning can affect you at any stage of life and is something that should be considered well in advance of retirement. There are tax-related questions you should be asking throughout your life:

• If you are, say, forty years old, are you contributing the maximum amount—or as much as you can afford—to your 401(k) plan or an IRA?

• Are you contributing at least something to a Roth IRA that will provide tax-free income later in life?

• Are you finding ways to structure the savings you are dedicating for your children's college education though tax advantageous plans such as state-sponsored 529 plans or the Coverdell education savings account?

• Do you have life insurance that will eventually pass on a tax-free death benefit to a surviving spouse or beneficiaries?

Taxes and tax planning are a part of all of these investment tools. Having a relationship with a financial services professional who works in conjunction with a CPA can help you build a truly comprehensive financial plan that not only works with your investments, but also shapes your assets to find the most efficient ways to prepare for tax time.

CHAPTER TEN

Different Bridges Cross the Same River:
The Roth IRA

Before he served as an Associate Justice on the United States Supreme Court from 1916 to 1939, Louis Brandeis was regarded as a fierce defender of public interests. He helped expand the "right to privacy" concept, and later fought against railroad monopolies, corporate corruption, and workplace abuses, often working on a pro bono basis so as not to be restricted in expressing his views. He played a role in establishing the Federal Reserve System and also offered ideas that led to the establishment of the Federal Trade Commission.

Prior to his nomination and heated confirmation to the nation's highest court, Brandeis authored a book, *Other People's Money and How Bankers Use It*. He once described his ideas on tax planning with this anecdote.[15]

"I live in Alexandria, Virginia. Near the Court Chambers, there is a toll bridge across the Potomac. When in a rush, I pay the dollar toll and get home early. However, I usually drive outside the downtown section of the city and cross the Potomac on a free bridge.

"The bridge was placed outside the downtown Washington, D.C. area to serve a useful social service—getting drivers to drive the extra mile and help alleviate congestion during the rush hour.

"If I went over the toll bridge and through the barrier without paying a toll, I would be committing tax evasion. If I drive the extra mile and drive outside the city of Washington to the free bridge, I am using a legitimate, logical and suitable method of tax avoidance, and I am performing a useful social service by doing so.

---

[15] "Louis D. Brandeis quotes," www.goodreads.com

"For my tax evasion, I should be punished. For my tax avoidance, I should be commended. The tragedy is that few people know that the free bridge exists."

Like Brandeis, most American taxpayers have options when it comes to "crossing the Potomac," which in the above analogy is another way of saying "paying your inevitable tax bill." It's a financial professional's job to tell you what options are available in finding the most tax-efficient way of doing so.

Sure, you can always wait until "tax season" in March or April to file your taxes. This is when you might pay someone to prepare your return, or buy tax preparation software that promises to offer every tax-saving break possible in the hope that you don't end up paying the government a large portion of your income. Or, you could instead work with your financial professional well in advance of tax reporting season and incorporate a tax plan, one that seeks to control and lower your future tax obligations as part of your overall financial planning strategy.

Filing later, to return to the Brandeis analogy, is like crossing the toll bridge. Tax planning is like crossing the free bridge. It takes some additional time and effort, but it can ultimately save you some money.

Which road would you rather take?

Most people can answer that question quickly and easily. Obviously, most people want to save money and pay less in taxes. What makes this situation really difficult in real life, however, is that the signs along the road directing us to the free bridge are often not that clear.

To most Americans, and even to plenty of professional people who have studied it, the U.S. tax code is overwhelming in detail—an easy road to get lost on. There are a seemingly endless number of rules and exceptions to rules, caveats, and conditions that are difficult to comprehend. This is where a professional financial planner, possibly working in conjunction with a certified public account, can help you better understand your tax planning options and the bottom-line impacts of those options.

THE TAX ADVANTAGEOUS ROTH IRA

One of the first tax planning strategies you might discuss is making the maximum use of the Roth IRA, which we touched on briefly in the previous chapter.

The Roth, by way of short summary, differs from the traditional IRA in that the Roth is funded by money that already has been taxed. This means that while withdrawals from traditional IRAs are taxed as ordinary income, distributions from Roth accounts are not taxed, provided certain conditions are met.[16] Moreover, required minimum distributions are not mandatory with a Roth as they are a traditional IRA. Better yet, a Roth can be passed tax free to heirs, and distributions from a Roth do not count as part of your provisional income that determines taxation on Social Security benefits.

The annual amount you can contribute to both a traditional IRA and a Roth is the same. In 2019 those contribution limits were $6,000 (or $7,000 if you were age fifty or older by the end of 2018). But unlike traditional IRAs that have no limit on how much you can earn and still make contributions, annual contributions to a Roth are limited by the investor's annual income.[17]

---

[16] *A qualified distributions from a Roth IRA can be excluded from gross income if a) it occurs at least five years after the first Roth contribution; b) if the account owner has reached age fifty-nine-and-a-half; c) if the account holder is disabled; or d) on or after the account holder's death.* Source: "Designated Roth Accounts: Distributions." www.irs.gov

[17] *A couple filing jointly or a qualifying widow(er) can make an annual Roth contribution if they have taxable compensation (wages, self-employment, commissions, alimony) and have a modified adjusted gross income (MAGI) less than $193,000. The amount of such contributions, however, is reduced for joint filers or a qualifying widow(er) with MAGI totals of more than $193,000 but less than $202,999. No contributions are allowed for income over $203,000. An IRS table computes the amount of reduction. A single filer, head of household, or married person filing separately can make an annual Roth contribution if they have MAGI of less than $122.000. However, that contribution amount is reduced for such persons with MAGI totals that exceed $122,000 but are less than $136,999. No contributions are allowed for income over $137,000.* Source: "Publication 590A: Contributions to Individual Retirement Accounts." www.irs.gov

The decision on how to invest for retirement—whether in a company-provided 401(k), a traditional IRA or in a Roth (or all three)—becomes a "pay me now or pay me later" question for many people,

For many younger workers with still-growing incomes and families, the question is easily answered. They generally need all the income they can get to pay bills, to feed and educate the kids, to provide both the basic necessities and, the occasional extra niceties of life. They often take immediate advantage of the tax deferral opportunities offered by 401(k) plans or traditional IRAs. Money contributed here is not part of that year's taxable income; it becomes a tax break. They gladly accept the notion that they will pay that tax someday, presumably in retirement when taxable income will likely be lower and the tax obligation less. Finding already taxed money for an additional Roth IRA contribution is often difficult in the early stages of our working careers.

The bigger question comes later in life.

This is the time when you start hearing and thinking about the impact of taxes in retirement—again, possibly the second biggest drain (behind medical costs) to a retirement nest egg. This is when you start hearing about the tax-free advantages of distributions from Roth accounts as well as the options of "Roth conversions." This is the process of transferring money out of a traditional IRA or 401(k)—an event that produces a taxable event on all money withdrawn—and into a Roth. Once this taxable conversion is made, the Roth money continues to grow until it is withdrawn tax free (provided certain conditions are met.) [18]

Whether to exercise a Roth conversion is another "pay now or later" proposition. You know your IRA or 401(k) money is going to be taxed someday, and you know that day will eventually be forced upon you when RMDs kick in at age seventy-two. You also know you will pay tax in any year you move money from a tax-deferred account into a Roth. So, you have the option to work with your financial professional, and possibly a CPA, to determine whether or when a Roth conversion might be done in a

---

[18] *A qualified distributions from a Roth IRA can be excluded from gross income if a) it occurs at least five years after the first Roth contribution; b) if the account owner has reached age fifty-nine-and-a-half; c) if the account holder is disabled; or d) on or after the account holder's death.* Source: "Designated Roth Accounts: Distributions." www.irs.gov

tax-efficient manner, one that doesn't elevate you into a higher tax bracket or affect the taxation of Social Security benefits.

There are a lot of elements to take into consideration when considering a Roth IRA conversion.

You need to know that the conversion amounts—the money you transfer out of your tax-deferred accounts—will be added to your taxable income in the year you do a conversion. This could produce a ripple effect on your overall tax structure for that year. It could cause a bump in your tax bracket, meaning you will pay a higher rate on your tax obligation. It will affect provisional income that determines how Social Security might be taxed. It's a fairly complex equation, and it should generally be handled with a financial professional who might also bring in a CPA who is part of, or works closely with, the advisor's firm.

Is there a prime age for doing such conversions?

There is not. You can't really recommend a target age because everyone's situation is different. Deciding whether or when to do a Roth conversion, as well as how much money to convert, involves knowing if you can do so at a level that maintains tax efficiency. That level is generally one that puts you near the top of your current tax bracket without being bumped into a higher one.

SOME ROTH CONVERSION STRATEGIES

The challenging situations we encounter in life often present us with strategic options when it comes to considering Roth conversions or any other occasion in which we might voluntarily take withdrawals from tax-deferred accounts.

You might, for example, have a year in which you have significant medical deductions, or incur losses from business operations or investments. Sorry to hear about your misfortune, but these events may present an opportunity to move assets out of your tax-deferred accounts. Another such opportunity might present itself in the first years of retirement when income earned from wages diminishes and you might be in a lower tax bracket.

Any event that decreases taxable income presents a chance to offset some or even all of the tax you will owe when taking money out of tax-deferred accounts. How you choose to use that money is up to you. Maybe you need it to pay unexpected expenses, or maybe you want to move it into a Roth IRA. Whatever the motivation, when you have the opportunity to do a taxable withdrawal in a year when your taxable income will be reduced, you should strongly consider it, as there will be other years when such a transfer will not be tax efficient.

Working with a CPA can often give you a better idea of how a Roth conversion might affect your overall tax structure. Most financial representatives have access to one or more CPAs with whom they work closely. In my Georgia practice, I work closely with two such accountants who are available to work with my clients, if requested.

Note here that you can make Roth conversions for any tax year up until April 15 of the following year. This gives you time to prepare your tax return and have a better understanding of how a Roth conversion credited to the previous year might affect your tax situation.

One other note.

It is my personal belief that, when doing a Roth IRA conversion or any withdrawal from a tax-deferred account, the taxes generated by the distribution should be paid from non-qualified funds as opposed to withholding the tax payment from the qualified funds being transferred.

Example: Let's say you are converting $100,000, and that will generate a tax liability of $15,000. It is my opinion that you should not cover the $15,000 in taxes by moving only $85,000 into the Roth. You instead should try to pay that tax obligation with "outside money," money generated by non-qualified, non-tax-deferred accounts. Maybe you've got some taxable money sitting in a bank account, or from an inheritance, or part of a severance package for early retirement. This is money that might be better used to pay the taxes on a conversion.

The challenge in doing a Roth conversion and paying the taxes out of the qualified money being transferred is the first percentage of all gains represents money you eventually pay in taxes. You pay, say, 15 percent in taxes, and whatever remains is often the point where you started. You almost lose the entire value of the tax-deferred growth.

On the other hand, paying taxes on Roth conversions with money transferred from the qualified account can work for people who are younger. Their tax liability is usually smaller, and they have a longer period of time to experience potential growth in the Roth account that can offset what they paid in taxes. But when you are close to or in retirement, I believe it is important to pay taxes for Roth conversions with other funds.

USING ROTH MONEY FOR LEVERAGE AND LEGACY PLANNING

Having the availability of tax-free Roth distributions can have several big-picture implications on your overall retirement plan.

Roth assets give you a source of income to 1) support your lifestyle while 2) effectively managing your withdrawals from your other taxable accounts. Example: You might avoid voluntarily taking taxable money from an IRA or 401(k) if you can take tax-free money from a Roth instead. Such a move can have a ripple effect across your tax structure in terms of both reducing overall taxable income as well as provisional income that determines Social Security taxation.

Bottom line: The more money you can put into a Roth now, the less you will pay in taxes later.

Don't overlook, either, the value a Roth IRA offers in its ability to be passed to heirs on a tax-free basis. This makes the inheritance consequences for a Roth vastly different from those of a traditional IRA.

A traditional IRA, as well as a 401(k), has tax consequence for whomever inherits it. Taxes are owed on these tax-deferred accounts, and somebody is going to have to pay them eventually.

Big differences apply when the IRA is inherited by a surviving spouse as opposed to non-spousal beneficiaries.

• Spouses who are the sole designated beneficiary can:[19]

• Treat an inherited IRA as their own, or

• Base RMDs on their own current age,

• Base RMDs on the decedent's age at death, reducing the distribution period by one each year, or

• Withdraw the entire account balance by the end of the tenth year following the account owner's death, provided the account owner died before the required beginning date to take RMDs. If the account owner

---

[19] "Retirement Topics: Required Minimum Distributions." www.irs.gov

died before the required beginning date, the surviving spouse can wait until the owner would have turned seventy-two to begin RMDs.

Non-spousal beneficiaries have fewer options. They cannot treat the inherited IRA as their own or make new contributions to it. They cannot roll over the inherited IRA into another tax-deferred vehicle. However, they do have choices. They can:

• Withdraw the entire account balance in a lump sum, paying all taxes owned in the year the lump sum distribution was taken.

• Withdraw the entire account balance by the end of the tenth year following the account owner's death, if the account owner died before beginning RMDs. Taxes are owed in each of the years distributions are taken.

• *If* they are fewer than ten years younger than the decedent or *if* they are disabled or chronically ill, a beneficiary may begin taking RMDs based on their own age and life expectancy, as determined by IRS tables. The RMD status of the deceased also affects distributions taken by the non-spousal beneficiary. If the deceased died *before* RMDs began, the beneficiary's age at year-end following the year of the owner's death determines the RMD. This number will increase each year as the beneficiary ages. If the deceased died *after* RMDs began, the RMD is the longer of 1) the beneficiary's remaining life expectancy, or 2) the owner's remaining life expectancy at the time of death. In order to use the lifetime RMD option, the beneficiary must begin taking distributions no later than December 31 of the year following the year of the owner's death. Failure to take this first RMD at the required time will dictate that the inherited IRA be liquidated in a five-year period.

Many of the same rules regarding inherited traditional IRAs also apply to inherited Roth IRAs. A Roth can't be held forever. The original Roth owner may not have to take withdrawals during their lifetime, but distributions must start upon the owner's death. How they are taken is determined by whether a surviving spouse or non-spousal beneficiaries receive the inherited Roth account.

As is the case with traditional IRAs, an inheriting spouse can take an inherited Roth and treat it as their own, rolling it over into their own account. Whether RMDs are required depends on the age of the deceased and the age of the survivor.

Non-spousal distributions, however, do incur RMDs. But this may not be a problem for the beneficiary. As the Roth IRA is inherited tax free, many people take the distribution immediately. Other people may elect to take only the required minimum distribution while leaving the balance to grow in order to establish a tax-free source of income whenever needed. This is the main difference between an inherited Roth IRA and a traditional one that comes with a tax obligation.

Still, rules on Roth distributions are easier to understand than those governing traditional IRAs, which is one reason I continue to believe in building up Roth IRA assets in whatever way you can best manage.

CHAPTER ELEVEN

Your Legacy: A Matter of Dollars and Sense

I t's not uncommon in my practice to encounter people who've made intelligent and well-developed retirement plans, yet who somehow overlook or delay the as-important task of legacy and estate planning.

I understand why, I truly do. Many of these otherwise forward-looking people believe there will always be time—just not today—to do estate planning. Many believe this right up to the point they unexpectedly run out of time. Others just aren't comfortable dealing with the idea of their own mortality. Who among us is?

In reality, these good folks already have an estate plan in place whether they know it or not. This default plan is not an especially good one, but it does provide a passing of assets from the deceased to loved ones, and sometimes even unloved ones. This plan is called probate, which we'll discuss in more detail here shortly. Probate will distribute your estate assets, but sometimes not in the way you intended.

"So, what's the big deal?" some might ask. "I don't have what you can really call an estate."

But that simply isn't true. Your name doesn't have to be Bezos or Buffett or Gates or Zuckerberg to have an estate. Everything you own at the time of death is part of an estate, big or small. Eventually, somebody is going to have to decide how everything in that estate is distributed.

We'll deal later in this chapter with estate-planning specifics such as probate, wills and trusts. But let's first address the concept of "legacy," something that involves more than the legal wrangling over how your earthly possessions will be divided after your passing.

Legacy is about building the memory people will have of you when you are gone. We all want those memories to be good ones, and that involves more than dollars and cents, heirlooms, family photos, property, trusts, and endowed scholarships. To be sure, part of how you will be remembered will be influenced by what you were able to do for others, but you don't need your name on a library or hospital wing to leave a legacy. Maybe you can provide assistance for your children in the purchase of a new home, or establish a college fund for grandchildren, or make a charitable grant to a local non-profit organization or foundation.

Or, your legacy might be shaped by the thoughtful and well-planned way you prepared for the distribution of your assets to loved ones or other entities that are important to you.

In my view, an important part of legacy planning involves simply paying enough attention to it.

This typically means taking the time to organize your important documents in one place where family members or a trusted someone has access to your various personal, legal, financial, or business records. It's making sure a lot of little details are updated and correct. It's checking to see you have beneficiaries designated the way you want on bank accounts, IRAs, brokerage accounts, insurance, and annuity policies. Are there ownership transfers in place to facilitate the sale of your home, cars, boats, or other personal property? Are there family heirlooms or other treasured items you want passed to specific individuals? Do you have power of attorney assigned to make decisions involving your everyday financial affairs or health care issues should you be unable to make those decisions for yourself? Have you designated custodians for minor children should something awful happen to you and a spouse?

The biggest part of any legacy or estate plan is caring for your family. Part of that involves money, but another part is helping your survivors through a very difficult transition at the time of your passing.

Here is where having a clear roadmap to your financial life and wishes is very important. Here is where having all your important information organized in one place will be most appreciated by heirs. Giving one or more trusted people the key to this "filing cabinet"—be it an actual storage place or a digital "cloud" location—makes a huge difference in organizing your affairs in an efficient manner when you are no longer in position to direct things.

We've all heard horror stories about spouses or adult children having to rummage through basement files for days looking for essential information, all the while wondering where their late spouse, father or mother could have possibly kept their will, their life insurance policy, the house title—any information their survivors suddenly had to have.

Legacy and estate planning also can come into play at times other than death. Such planning should be completed before a health emergency strikes and leaves you incapacitated and unable to express your wishes. This planning certainly should be done at a time when one is mentally capable of making such decisions. Remember, the mental health of an estate grantor is often one of the first things challenged when a will is contested in probate court.

The key here is determining, while you are still able to do so, the distribution of assets—financial and otherwise—in the manner of your choosing. Without a plan and instructions in place, that distribution might pass from your hands into those of government agencies—the IRS comes immediately to mind—or the courts.

The best way to get started on legacy and estate planning is to 1) draw up the determination to begin the process, and 2) consult professionals who should include your financial representative as well as an attorney with a background in estate planning. Let them guide you through the detailed and sometimes challenging process of dictating the distribution of your life's assets when you are no longer here to use them, and do so in a way that will leave your survivors with an appreciation of your final gift.

PREPARING YOUR LEGACY: TODS, WILLS AND TRUSTS

I occasionally hear people say that not everyone absolutely has to have a will. They will suggest that people whose financial assets are relatively simple—a bank account, an insurance policy or two, no home ownership or other significant personal property—might be able to get by on simple transfer-on-death (TOD) documents, as well as making desired beneficiary designations on insurance or annuity policies,

This may be true for some people. I strongly suspect, however, that most readers of this book have financial affairs that are not that simple. Most readers, like most of my clients, likely have financial assets that make the development of a will a bare necessity.

Most readers and clients know at least some of the consequences of dying without a will or trust in place. To pass without having legal documents establishing your wishes is to die intestate. This is when a probate court will decide the distribution of your assets because you neglected to do so.

A will is an important and useful legal document that should be part of your legacy planning. It may not, however, be the most efficient way to distribute your assets. Consider the potential for problems with 1) probate and 2) unintentional disinheritance.

PROBLEM #1: PROBATE

Probate has a bad reputation that is often well deserved. It has the potential to be a costly, time-consuming process that might diminish your estate and delay the distribution of your assets to loved ones. In some states, this can be a truly nasty process indeed. Unless you have made a clear plan for avoiding probate—some options for which we'll discuss soon—it is possible that you have assets that will pass through probate. Beyond that, if your will and beneficiary designations aren't correctly structured, some of these assets will go through a probate process that has the potential to turn dollars into cents.

It is equally possible, however, that probate can be something less than a frustrating, costly process. If you have a properly drawn will, probate is often just a formality and there is little risk that your will won't be executed per your instructions. Whether the probate process is relatively simple or more complex often depends on the state in which the process is conducted. Some states have very difficult probate processes; others do not. My home state of Georgia, for instance, is very probate-friendly. It's relatively easy here. But Texas can be very difficult, and the entire Northeast can be that way.

Most probate problems arise when the will is challenged, a process that brings additional costs and a possibly lengthy timeline into play.

Such challenges can come from anywhere. They could come from family members unhappy with the way you chose to distribute assets, or changes you made to your original will. They could come from people with claims against your estate. They could come from people with claims against those who will inherit from your estate. Some of these claims may be valid, others may not be. But because all probate court issues are a matter of public record, and because all wills must be validated by a probate court, anyone can see the contents of a will being probated and challenge it.

Keep in mind, too, that a probate court may have to become involved while you are still alive. Should you become physically or mentally incapacitated without making any prior designation for the handling of your business or health care affairs, or for the custody of minor children, a probate court may have to make those decisions on your behalf.

Probate proceedings can be notoriously expensive, and often lengthy and ponderous. A typical probate process identifies all of your assets and debts. It then pays from the estate assets any taxes and court fees that you owe (including estate taxes) before distributing the remaining property and assets to your inheritors. This process can sometimes take at least a year or even longer in some states. Add in the sometimes-exorbitant fees that may be charged by lawyers and accountants during the process and you can see where probate has the potential to be an expensive proposition.

PROBLEM #2: UNINTENTIONALLY DISINHERITING YOUR FAMILY

You would never want to unintentionally disinherit loved ones because of confusion surrounding your legacy plan. Unfortunately, it happens. Why? This terrible situation is typically caused by a simple lack of understanding. In particular, mistakes regarding legacy distribution occur with regards to those whom people care for most: their grandchildren.

One of the most important ways to plan for the inheritance of your grandchildren is by properly structuring the distribution of your legacy. Specifically, you need to determine whether your legacy will be distributed on a per stirpes or per capita bases.

Per stirpes is a legal term that in Latin means "by the branch." Your estate will be distributed per stirpes if you designate each branch of your family to receive an equal share of your estate. In the event that your children predecease you, their share will be distributed evenly between their children—your grandchildren.

With per capita distribution, you may designate different amounts of your estate to be distributed to members of the same generation.

Per stirpes distribution of assets will follow the family tree down the line as the predecessor beneficiaries pass away. On the other hand, per capita distribution of assets ends on the branch of the family tree with the death of a designated beneficiary. For example, when your child passes away in a per capita distribution, their children would not receive distributions from the assets that you designated to your child.

A simple way to remember the difference between the two types of distribution goes something like this:

"Stirpes are forever, and Capita is capped."

What the terms mean is not nearly as important as what they do. The reality is that improperly titled assets could accidentally leave your grandchildren disinherited upon the death of their parents. It's easy to check, and even easier to fix. But again, this is an example of how attention to details is so important in legacy planning

ALTERNATIVES TO PROBATE

Probate can be a painstakingly public process. Because the probate process happens in court, the assets you own that go through a probate procedure become part of the public record. While this may not seem like a big deal to some, other people don't want that kind of intimate information available to the public.

Additionally, if your estate is entirely distributed via your will, the money that your family may need to cover the costs of your medical bills, funeral expenses, and estate taxes could be tied up in probate. While family members may have the option of requesting cash from your probated assets to cover immediate health care expenses, taxes, and fees, that process comes with its own set of complications.

This is why choosing alternative methods for distributing your legacy assets might make life easier for your loved ones and help them claim more of your estate in a timely fashion.

A simpler and less tedious approach is to avoid probate altogether by structuring your estate to be distributed outside of the probate process. Two common ways of doing this are by structuring your assets inside a life insurance plan, which we'll discuss in more detail later in this chapter. One might also use individual retirement planning tools like IRAs that give you the option of designating a beneficiary(s) upon your death.

Then, there is always the trust option.

The issue of "will vs. trust" is a debate often heard among estate planning professionals, be they lawyers or financial advisors. I'm not advocating either option here. There is a place for either or both, depending on an individual's specific estate distributions wishes as well as the state in which the estate planning is done. Generally speaking, while I'm not big on always recommending a trust, I do believe most of my clients should have a will at the very least.

There are definite advantages to establishing a trust, a slightly more expensive and detailed process than the drawing up of a will.

Assets included in a trust are not subject to the probate process and are not a matter of public record.

Assets in a trust typically can be passed on in a timely manner. In most cases, a designated trustee need only show a certificate of death to gain control of the assets placed in the trust by the deceased trustor(s)—the person or persons who originally established the trust.

A trust establishes separate durable power of attorney for both business affairs and health care matters. These powers take effect only if the trustor(s) become incapacitated or otherwise incapable of making decisions. These powers disappear upon the death of the trustor, at which point all control of the assets pass to the designated trustee(s).

Assets in a trust are not subject to claims sought by creditors.

Let's note briefly here the big difference in two types of trusts.

A "revocable" trust is one that, as the name implies, can be changed anytime by the person or persons who established it. These are the "trustors" or "grantors" of the trust. They also are the first "trustees," meaning they have full access to and control of all assets within the trust during their lifetime. When one spouse passes, the surviving spouse becomes the sole trustee. When the survivor dies, control of the trust passes to a successor trustee(s) designated by the grantors. Successor trustees can be one or more family members; an institution (such as a bank's trust department or a charitable foundation); or a trusted friend who will oversee all distributions from the trust. All trustees are legally obligated to follow the wishes of the grantors when making distributions.

An "irrevocable" trust is one that, once put in place, cannot be altered even by the trustor or grantor.

Deciding how to pass on your assets in the most efficient way possible—whether through transfer-on-death designations, a will, a trust or any other estate planning strategy—is something you need to discuss with an attorney experienced in estate matters. It is often helpful if this attorney has a relationship with your financial professional, as the two should eventually work together to determine whether all your assets are included in a will or correctly titled within a trust.

Let's now look more closely at one more legacy-planning option, one that does not entail wills, trusts, or probate.

LIFE INSURANCE AS A LEGACY TOOL

Another way to avoid complicated legacy distribution problems, as well as the probate process, is by leveraging a life insurance plan.

Life insurance is a tool that can be used to achieve specific things at different times of our lives. When we were young and likely needed every penny we earned to pay the everyday expenses of a growing family, we might have purchased term insurance. It was relatively cheap, and it served a specific purpose: providing essential income to a young family should its principal wage earner pass away. But it only served that purpose for a designated period of time, hence the name "term insurance." If you didn't use it during the period of coverage—and I'm assuming you didn't, or you wouldn't be reading this—you received no monetary value from the premiums you paid.

As you move into retirement, however, the needs for life insurance change. Your goals now are different and likely involve creating a source of income that will support a surviving spouse for as long as they live. Term insurance is no longer appropriate, as you don't want a term policy expiring shortly before you do.

A second goal in retirement might be legacy giving. In this area, life insurance has some very interesting possibilities.

Permanent life insurance, in contrast to term, comes with the guarantee to pay a death benefit to somebody, someday. Moreover, this payment will be made on a tax-free basis.

Consider the leverage options of the investment tool we just described.

I often meet with people who would like to leave something behind for their families but wonder how to do it. Their first consideration is, "Are we going to be able to financially survive retirement and do some of the things we want to do without running out of money?" They also want to provide something for heirs, but they know they must provide for themselves first.

Life insurance has the potential to address both goals. It can be used in such a way that the insured doesn't have to compromise their lifestyle just to make sure their family is provided for when they are gone. A life insurance policy can address income concerns for a surviving spouse. Should the survivor not need the death benefit, it can provide a legacy benefit for contingent beneficiaries in future generations.

Let's say you have a goal of leaving $100,000 to your daughter and her children. The first way of doing that, of course, is to save $100,000. But another way might be to leverage $20,000 in a life insurance policy that at the time of your passing will pay her a tax-free $100,000 death benefit. The $80,000 you did not have to generate to meet your legacy goal is essentially money available for your retirement.

Another thing I hear often is, "I'm seventy years old. Why do I need life insurance?"

The answer is, you may not need it, but that can depend on a lot of different factors. What are you trying to accomplish? Are you trying to provide guaranteed income for a surviving spouse, or for adult children or grandchildren? Are you healthy enough to even qualify for life insurance? Will the amount of premiums you pay at this late stage of your life generate a death benefit that makes fiscal sense?

If leaving something for future generations is not especially important to you, life insurance becomes a less attractive tool in retirement. It's probably something that's not needed. But if you want a legacy gift, especially one that does not compromise your own lifestyle, life insurance can be a pretty good tool. It allows you to leverage a smaller amount of money into a potentially bigger pool of tax-free money that will be available to a loved one, or several loved ones, after you pass.

Another important aspect to remember when considering life insurance as a legacy tool: The tax-free death benefit is shielded from probate, and a creditor cannot make a claim against a death benefit.

On a more cautionary note, a person using life insurance as a legacy tool should understand that beneficiary designations in a life insurance policy supersede instructions made in a will. In other words, if your will calls for all assets to be split between two children, but your insurance policy only lists one as a beneficiary, the policy's death benefit goes only to the designated child. You need to make sure your will and insurance policies are, so to speak, on the same page.

One final note of caution. Paying premiums on a life insurance policy should always be regarded as an investment in the future; in this case, the future of your family. Like all investments, insurance premiums should be paid with funds available only after all other essential expenses are met. This is especially important in retirement.

THE LIVING BENEFITS OF LIFE INSURANCE

I mentioned earlier how life insurance can offer leverage possibilities, which is a fancy way of describing something that can help achieve multiple goals.

One leverage option is the "living benefits" offered by some life insurance policies and annuity contracts. This option—not available in all policies or states—allows the insured to use a portion of the death benefit while still alive. This living benefits option is typically an add-on rider available for an additional fee.

Let's look more closely at how this works and why it might be an option to consider. One of the things most likely to derail retirement planning is a prolonged illness that might require expensive long-term care, either via at-home options or in a long-term care facility.

Purchasing long-term care insurance is one way of addressing this concern, but it's not always the best option. This coverage can be very expensive, and the premiums are likely to increase over time. It also can be a use-it-or-lose-it proposition, though not always. (Some long-term care policies now offer return-of-premium options on unused policies.) The reliability of some insurance companies issuing long-term care policies can also be a concern, as some have been known to simply disappear or sell their accounts to someone else and move on to a different business.

With these concerns in mind, many people in retirement struggle to find ways to finance the likely prospect of incurring health care costs that are growing between 4.5 and 5 percent a year—a rate double that of inflation. That means health care costs are doubling every thirteen to fifteen years, and anyone near or in retirement has to have a plan to deal with that.[20]

Many traditional life insurance policies today offer alternatives to a straight long-term care insurance policy by offering life insurance with living benefits riders. A living benefit allows you to use a percentage of the policy's death benefit for health care expenses while you are still alive. Important note: Exercising this option reduces the death benefit available to beneficiaries. Some annuities also make this kind of add-on option available to help cover health care costs. The living benefit trigger is typically a life-changing event such as chronic, critical, or terminal illness.

These benefits generally won't cover all of one's health care costs, but they certainly help. Some can help cover expensive nursing home care, should the insured be deemed incapable of performing any two of six activities of daily living (ADLs)—bathing, eating, dressing, toileting, transferring (the ability to get out of a bed or chair without assistance), and maintaining continence. Other living benefits might assist in covering the costs of at-home care.

Keep in mind, too, that long-term nursing care or memory care is not covered by Medicare. Some coverage is available through Medicaid, the government's health care program for people with incomes below a certain threshold. It should be noted, however, that qualifying for Medicaid coverage can be a difficult process in which an applicant must show a history—usually a few years' worth—of having very limited assets.

Clearly then, providing for long-term care is something we should expect to finance on our own. How you do this is up to you.

---

[20] Peter G. Peterson Foundation. May 1, 2019. " Healthcare Costs for Americans Projected to Grow at an Alarmingly High Rate." https://www.pgpf.org/blog/2019/05/healthcare-costs-for-americans-projected-to-grow-at-an-alarmingly-high-rate

Sure, you can set out to self-finance your future health care by saving for that expressed purpose. Any dollar you put into (and any return generated by) an investment account, savings account or Health Savings Account (HSA) can be earmarked for future health care needs. Human nature being what it is, this might require a good deal of mental discipline to not spend that set-aside money prematurely, but it is one option.

Another is to consider the life insurance options described previously that can leverage premiums into a bigger pool of money that will 1) pay a death benefit to a surviving spouse or future generations, and 2) provide at least some assistance in financing expensive late-in-life nursing care.

Another insurance option is an annuity with an income rider or some type of enhanced death benefit which may increase the value of the inherited assets. As explained in our previous discussion of annuities, your invested principal (the premium paid to purchase the annuity) can be contractually guaranteed to grow by a fixed annual percentage. That rising income value will determine the level of income you will receive when you choose to begin receiving it. This income can be used for any desired purpose such as retirement expenses, legacy giving, or paying health care costs. Moreover, an annuity that offers living benefits gives you another option to help pay health care expenses.

The option you choose is entirely up to you. But in the preceding options, you have the choice between 1) employing the self-discipline required to invest and ride out the ups and downs of the market, or 2) leveraging money via insurance tools that contractually guarantee future income that can be used for multiple purposes, among them legacy giving and paying for health care.

One other note on life insurance options: Most plans require that you be medically qualified to get life insurance, so it is better to apply for insurance sooner than later, when you might have medical conditions that will deter the insurance company from insuring you.

USING IRAS FOR LEGACY GIVING

Don't overlook the legacy implications of IRAs, as described in the previous chapter.

Yes, inherited IRAs have tax implications, but they allow for the asset to pass to designated beneficiaries who will not be subject to the probate process. Remember, too, that inheriting beneficiaries have a few options on how they receive, and pay taxes on, the IRA money you leave them.

How your heirs receive and pay taxes on the legacy gift you leave is mostly up to them. Maybe you don't care what they do with your money. You, sadly, won't be around to see it.

FINAL THOUGHTS ON LEGACY PLANNING: GET PROFESSIONAL HELP

There is more to your legacy than your property, money, investments, and other assets you leave to family members, loved ones, and charities.

Everyone has a legacy beyond money. You also leave behind personal items of importance, your values and beliefs, your personal and family history, and your wishes. You need to make these wishes known, preferably through a will or other legal means. When it comes time for your family and loved ones to make decisions after you are gone, knowing your wishes can help them make decisions that honor you and your legacy as well as give meaning to what you leave behind.

Your financial professional and an attorney with a background in estate planning can help you organize your affairs and execute your wishes in the way you want. Among other things, they will help you pay proper attention to details that often get overlooked amid the flurry of daily living. Among them:

• Are your assets actually titled and held the way you think they are?

• Are your beneficiaries set up the way you think they should be?

• Have there been changes to your family or those you desire as beneficiaries?

• Is information on all your financial, business and legal affairs in a place where loved ones can easily find it?

• Have you made provisions for the distribution of personal items of emotional significance?

• Does the plan truly reflect the values you held in life and the memories you hope to leave behind you?

This can be complicated stuff, but it is extremely important that you have at least a basic understanding of its various components. This doesn't mean you must understand all the legalese involved; this is why you hire an attorney and an advisor. But you should know at least enough to explain to potential heirs the basics of your plan and how it will someday affect them. You should also understand how to make changes to the plan, if necessary. Changes in either your life or the lives of your heirs—death, divorce, illness, sudden unemployment—might necessitate change in your legacy planning.

One final thing to consider.

Taking the time to formulate an estate plan—whether done through a will, trust or other means—involves financial housekeeping that will be much appreciated by loved ones in the difficult days and weeks immediately following your passing. This is the time when they must do the unpleasant but necessary task of locating essential documents—financial accounts, insurance policies, pension information, deeds, car titles, debts owed, professional, and personal contacts. Organizing and making this material available to those you cared for most in life is a service you can offer while alive.

Consider it part of your final gift, one that can help shape positive memories when you are gone. Part of how you will be remembered—in addition to the love you gave, the hard work and good deeds you performed, the funny or even embarrassing memories you leave behind—will also include the way you leave your affairs to those who follow you.

No amount of inherited assets will ease the pain on the occasion of a family member's passing, but fond memories of a life well-lived often help in the grieving process. Financial assets may come and go, but pleasant memories of loved ones usually last a lifetime.

CHAPTER TWELVE

Choosing a Financial Professional

From the moment you dip your toes into the retirement planning pool to the point you start swimming laps—with your assets organized, your income needs met, and your accumulation and legacy plans in place—working with a professional you trust can make all the difference in how well your retirement reflects your desires.

It is important to know what you are looking for before taking the plunge. There are many people who would love to handle your money, but not everyone is capable of structuring a truly holistic retirement strategy.

The distinction to be made here is that you should look for someone who puts your interests first and actively wants to help you meet your goals and objectives. Oftentimes, the products someone sells you matter less than that professional's dedication to making sure you have a plan that meets your needs.

A true professional will take your whole financial position into consideration, adjust your risk exposure, and help you with tools and strategies that secure your desired income during retirement. They can create investment strategies that allow you to continue accumulating wealth during your retirement for you to use later on or that can contribute to your legacy.

Financial products and investment tools change, but the concepts that lie behind wise retirement planning are lasting. In the end, a good financial professional's approach is designed for and around those serious about planning for retirement.

It's easy to see how choosing a financial professional can be one of the most important decisions you make in your life. Not only do they provide you with advice, they also manage the personal assets that supply your retirement income and contribute to your legacy.

So, how do you find a good one?

DECIDE WITH WHAT TYPE OF PROFESSIONAL YOU WANT TO WORK

There are three basic kinds of financial professionals, though many professionals may play overlapping roles. It is important to know a professional's primary function as well as how they charge for their services and whether they are obligated to act in your best interest.

Registered Representatives, better known as stockbrokers or bank / investment representatives, make their living by earning commissions on investment services. Stockbrokers basically sell you investment products. The products from which they make the highest commission are sometimes the products they recommend to their clients. If you want to make a simple transaction, such as buying or selling a particular stock, a Registered Representative can help you.

Insurance agents earn commissions on the insurance products they sell. Oftentimes they call themselves advisors or planners, but they are generally limited to offering only insurance-based products. These agents can be helpful for satisfying insurance needs, but if you are interested in exploring your options beyond insurance, you will likely benefit by considering advisors who can offer more comprehensive options.

Investment Advisor Representatives, the group to which I belong, are unique in that we can offer any number of investment options. An Investment Advisor Representative may provide more comprehensive financial advice and is compensated on a fee basis. They are often independent, meaning they are not held captive by the products or investment philosophy of any one company or group. They do, however, often have licensure as stockbrokers or insurance agents, allowing them to earn commissions on certain transactions. More importantly, if they are financial professionals as I am, they are held to high ethical standards and are required to make financial decisions in your best interest and reflecting your risk tolerance in advisory accounts as well as in retirement accounts. They are not focused on individual stocks, investments, or markets. They look at the big picture, the whole enchilada. An Investment Advisor Representative can also help you with non-financial aspects of your legacy by coordinating with estate planning professionals and tax professionals to build a comprehensive strategy designed to help you save money.

THE SELECTION PROCESS: DO YOUR DILIGENCE, THEN TRUST YOUR GUT

Books such as this one often conclude with chapters (such as this one) on how to choose a financial representative. Such chapters typically offer detailed advice about choosing from a list of several candidates, asking questions about the investment and retirement planning philosophies of each, checking out their credentials, requesting references and inquiring about how they receive compensation.

I have no problem with any of this advice, all of which can be part of the information gathering process. But I also believe that some of my professional peers tend to describe this decision-making process in far too much detail, sometimes making it seem like a formidable task.

I believe there is a better way to find a financial professional who is right for you. I would summarize the process in a few simple words:

Do your diligence. Then trust your gut.

To be sure, you will want to interview any financial professional before deciding whether this person is the one to help guide you along the journey to and through retirement. And you may need to visit with more than one candidate before finding the person with whom you feel most comfortable.

I would suggest finding this level of trust, comfort and confidence is as important, if not more so, than checking a prospective advisor's professional credentials or a selectively edited list of recommendations. This need not be an overly analytical process. Your gut will usually tell you whether the professional you are considering is one who shares your values, understands your goals and can develop a plan to realize them.

In short, you want to "click" with the person or company you choose. I've never seen a financial advisor who is a perfect fit for every client, and that certainly includes me. But you can find someone who is qualified, who speaks your language and is willing to spend the time necessary to ensure that you completely understand your retirement plan.

Establishing whether the professional you are considering has a responsible to clients is certainly part of the process. Inquiring about how they are compensated, whether on a fee basis or commission, is also part of the process.

Other parts of the decision-making process are more subjective. Do you believe this candidate has a genuine interest in you and your needs? Was this candidate a good listener or a non-stop talker? Is this someone who will return your calls and answer your questions? Is this someone you can trust with your financial future?

Clearly, these are questions that must be addressed subjectively, and there are no guidelines I cannot help you answer them other than to suggest that your own instincts will likely provide the best answers.

THE IMPORTANCE OF INDEPENDENCE

Not all investment firms and financial professionals are created equal. My hope is that the information in this book has demonstrated that leveraging investments for income and accumulation in today's frequently volatile market often requires a different way of looking at things. In short, you need innovative ideas to come up with the creative solutions that will provide you with the retirement that you want.

Innovation thrives on independence. No matter how good a financial professional is, the firm they represent needs to operate on principles that make sense in today's economy. Remember, advice about money has been around forever. Good advice, however, changes with the times.

Timing the market, relying on the sale of stocks for income and banking on high Treasury and bond returns are not strategies. They aren't even realistic ways to make money or generate income.

Working with an independent advisor can help you break free from the traditional ways of thinking and position you to create a realistic retirement plan. Working with an independent professional who relies on fee-based income may also give you greater peace of mind. When you do well, they do well, and that's the way it should be. Your independent financial professional will make sure that:

• Your assets are organized and structured to reflect your risk tolerance.

• Your assets will be available to you when you need them, and in the way that you need them.

• You will have a lifetime income that will support your lifestyle through your retirement.

- You are handling your taxes as efficiently as possible.
- Your legacy is in order.

Finding, interviewing, and selecting a financial professional can seem like a daunting task. And honestly, it may take a good amount of work to narrow the field and find the one you want. In the end, it is worth the effort. Your retirement, lifestyle, assets, and legacy are all on the line. The choices you make today will have lasting impacts on your life and the lives of your loved ones. Working with someone you trust and know you can rely on to help you make decisions that will benefit you is invaluable. The work it takes to find such a person is something you will never regret.

ABOUT THE AUTHOR

Tom Gandolfi is an entrepreneur and financial professional who seeks to provide objective information to help his clients achieve their retirement goals.

He comes to the financial industry from the other side of the desk as the former client of a brokerage firm where he spent years receiving financial and investment advice as the owner of his own marketing business. Stung by the market-related losses incurred by many Americans (including himself) during the dot-com bubble burst in 2000, he set out to *Find a Better Way* of investing, building and perhaps most importantly, protecting personal wealth in retirement.

He eventually decided that what he had learned through personal experience and research could be of great benefit to others looking for a better way to manage their financial future. He consequently founded Three Bridges Financial Group, an investment advisory firm keenly focused on retirement planning.

Since founding the firm, Gandolfi and his team have worked closely with individuals, families and couples to build and manage goal-based retirement plans specifically designed to help clients achieve their vision for the future. He believes in listening to the specific goals and needs of his clients, then working to explain and simplify the often-complex world of financial matters so his clients can make informed decisions as they plan for what should be the best years of their lives in retirement.

Today Gandolfi is a Investment Advisor Representative and has passed the Series 65 securities exam. He also holds a life and health insurance license in numerous states and is a member of the National Ethics Board. Tom and his wife, Sherri, have lived in the North Metro Atlanta area for over thirty years and have two young adult daughters, Tori and Kasey. He is very proud of his family and loves spending time with them. In addition to family vacations, Tom also enjoys golf, baseball, college football, and politics. He models his personal and professional life around the words of a very smart man:

"There's a way to do it better—find it."—Thomas Edison

GLOSSARY

To fully arm yourself with knowledge and enter into the foray of retirement strategies involves understanding the sometimes jargon-filled financial speak of the industry. To help you navigate the dense terminology, I have included this glossary.

ANNUAL RESET *(ANNUAL RATCHET, CLIQUET)**—Crediting methods measuring index movement over a one-year period. Positive interest is calculated and credited at the end of each contract year and cannot be lost if the index subsequently declines. Say that the index increased from 100 to 110 in one year and the indexed annuity had an 80 percent participation rate. The insurance company would take the 10 percent gross index gain for the year, apply the participation rate (10 percent index gain x 80 percent rate) and credit 8 percent interest to the annuity. What if in the following year the index declined back to 100? The individual would keep the 8 percent interest earned and simply receive zero interest that year. An annual reset structure preserves credited gains and treats negative index periods as years with zero growth.[21]

ANNUITANT—The person, usually the annuity owner, whose life expectancy is used to calculate the income payment on the annuity.

ANNUITY—An annuity is a contract issued by an insurance company that often serves as a type of savings plan with the goal of future income. It is used by individuals looking for long-term growth and protection of assets that will likely be needed within retirement.

AVERAGING—Index values may either be measured from a start point to an end point (point-to-point) or values between the start point and end point may be averaged to determine an ending value. Index values may be averaged over the days, weeks, months or quarters of the period.

---

[21] FixedAnnuityFacts.com. NAFA, the National Association for Fixed Annuities. November 12, 2013. "Glossary of Terms."

BENEFICIARY—A beneficiary is the person designated to receive payments due upon the death of the annuity owner or the annuitant themselves or retirement account owner.

BONUS RATE—A bonus rate is the "extra" or "additional" interest paid during the first year (the initial guarantee period), typically used as an incentive to get consumers to select one annuity policy over another.

CALL OPTION *(ALSO SEE PUT OPTION)*—Gives the holder the right to buy an underlying security or index at a specified price on or before a given date.

CAP—The maximum interest rate that will be credited to an annuity for the year or period. The cap usually refers to the maximum interest credited after applying the participation rate or yield spread. If the index methodology showed a 20 percent increase, the participation rate was 60 percent and the maximum interest cap was 10 percent, the contract would credit 10 percent interest. A few annuities use a maximum gain cap instead of a maximum interest cap, with the participation rate or yield spread applied to the lesser of the gain or the cap. If the index methodology showed a 20 percent increase and a contract's participation rate was 60 percent and the maximum gain cap was 10 percent, the contract would credit 6 percent interest.

COMPOUND INTEREST—Interest is earned on both the original principal and on previously earned interest. It is more favorable than simple interest. Suppose that your original principal was $1 and your interest rate was 10 percent for five years. With simple interest, your value is ($1 + $0.10 interest each year) = $1.50. With compound interest, your value is ($1 x 1.10 x 1.10 x 1.10 x 1.10 x 1.10) = $1.61. The advantage of compound interest over simple interest becomes greater as each subsequent period passes.

CREDITING METHOD *(ALSO SEE METHODOLOGY)*—The formula(s) used to determine the excess interest that is credited above the minimum interest guarantee.

DEATH BENEFITS—The payment the annuity owner's estate or beneficiaries will receive if he or she dies before the annuity matures. On most annuities, this is equal to the current account value. Some annuities offer an enhanced value at death via an optional rider that has a monthly or annual fee associated with it.

EXCESS INTEREST—Interest credited to the annuity contract above the minimum guaranteed interest rate. In an indexed annuity the excess interest is determined by applying a stated crediting method to a specific index or indices.

FIXED ANNUITY—A contract issued by an insurance company guaranteeing a minimum interest rate with the crediting of excess interest determined by the performance of the insurer's general account. Index annuities are fixed annuities.

FIXED DEFERRED ANNUITY—With fixed annuities, an insurance company offers a guaranteed interest rate plus safety of your principal and earnings (subject to the claims-paying ability of the insurance company). Your interest rate will be reset periodically, based on economic and other factors, but is guaranteed to never fall below a certain rate.

FREE WITHDRAWALS—Withdrawals that are free of surrender charges, or withdrawals made within the accepted terms of a contract.

INDEX—The underlying external benchmark upon which the crediting of excess interest is based, also a measure of the prices of a group of securities.

IRA (INDIVIDUAL RETIREMENT ACCOUNT)—An IRA is a tax-advantaged personal savings plan that lets an individual set aside money for retirement. All or part of the participant's contributions may be tax deductible, depending on the type of IRA chosen and the participant's personal financial circumstances. Distributions from many employer-sponsored retirement plans may be eligible to be rolled into an IRA to continue tax-deferred growth until the funds are needed. An annuity can be used as an IRA; that is, IRA funds can be used to purchase an annuity.

IRA ROLLOVER—IRA rollover is the phrase used when an individual who has a balance in an employer-sponsored retirement plan transfers that balance into an IRA. Such an exchange, when properly handled, is a tax-advantaged transaction.

LIQUIDITY—The ease with which an asset is convertible to cash. An asset with high liquidity provides flexibility, in that the owner can easily convert it to cash at any time, but it also tends to decrease profitability.

MARKET RISK—The risk of an asset's market value fluctuating over time. In a fixed or fixed indexed annuity, the original principal and credited interest are not subject to market risk. Even if the index declines, the annuity owner would receive no less than their original principal back if they decided to cash in the policy at the end of the surrender period. Unlike a security, indexed annuities guarantee the original premium and the premium is backed by, and is as safe as, the insurance company that issued it (subject to the claims-paying ability of the insurance company).

METHODOLOGY *(ALSO SEE CREDITING METHOD)*—The way that interest crediting is calculated. On fixed indexed annuities, there are a variety of different methods used to determine how index movement becomes interest credited.

MINIMUM GUARANTEED RETURN *(MINIMUM INTEREST RATE)*—Fixed indexed annuities typically provide a minimum guaranteed return over the life of the contract. At the time that the owner chooses to terminate the contract, the cash surrender value is compared to a second value calculated using the minimum guaranteed return and the higher of the two values is paid to the annuity owner.

OPTION—A contract which conveys to its holder the right, but not the obligation, to buy or sell something at a specified price on or before a given date. After this given date the option ceases to exist. Insurers typically buy options to provide for the excess interest potential. Options may be American style, whereby they may be exercised at any time prior to the given date, or they may have to be exercised only during a specified window. Options that may only be exercised during a specified period are European-style options.

OPTION RISK—Most insurers create the potential for excess interest in an indexed annuity by buying options. Say you could buy a share of stock for $50. If you bought the stock and it rose to $60, you could sell it for a $10 profit. But, if the stock price fell to $40, you'd have a $10 loss. Instead of buying the actual stock, we could buy an option that gave us the right to buy the stock for $50 at any time over the next year. The cost of the option is $2. If the stock price rose to $60, we would exercise our option, buy the stock at $50 and make $10 (less the $2 cost of the option).

If the price of the stock fell to $40, $30 or $10, we wouldn't use the option and it would expire. The loss is limited to $2—the cost of the option.

PARTICIPATION RATE—The percentage of positive index movement credited to the annuity. If the index methodology determined that the index increased 10 percent and the indexed annuity participated in 60 percent of the increase, it would be said that the contract has a 60 percent participation rate. Participation rates may also be expressed as asset fees or yield spreads.

POINT-TO-POINT—A crediting method measuring index movement from an absolute initial point to the absolute end point for a period. Example: An index had a period starting value of 100 and a period ending value of 120. A point-to-point method would record a positive index movement of 20 percent. Point-to-point usually refers to annual periods; however, the phrase is also used instead of term end point to refer to multiple year periods.

PREMIUM BONUS—Additional money that is credited to the accumulation account of an annuity policy under certain conditions.

PUT OPTION *(ALSO SEE CALL OPTION)*—Gives the holder the right to sell an underlying security or index at a specified price on or before a given date.

QUALIFIED ANNUITIES *(QUALIFIED MONEY)*—Qualified annuities are annuities purchased for funding an IRA, 403(b) tax-deferred annuity or other type of retirement arrangements. An IRA or qualified retirement plan provides the tax deferral. An annuity contract should be used to fund an IRA or qualified retirement plan to benefit from an annuity's features other than tax deferral, including the safety features, lifetime income payout option and death benefit protection.

REQUIRED MINIMUM DISTRIBUTION (RMD)—The amount of money that traditional, SEP and SIMPLE IRA owners and qualified plan participants must begin distributing from their retirement accounts by April 1 following the year they reach age seventy-two. RMD amounts must then be distributed each subsequent year.

RETURN FLOOR—*See Minimum Guaranteed Return*

ROTH IRA—Like other IRA accounts, the Roth IRA is simply a holding account that manages your stocks, bonds, annuities, mutual funds, and CDs. However, future withdrawals (including earnings and interest) are typically tax-free once the account has been open for five years and the account holder is age fifty-nine-and-one-half.

RULE OF 72—Tells you approximately how many years it takes a sum to double at a given rate. It's handy to be able to figure out, without using a calculator, that when you're earning a 6 percent return, for example, by dividing 6 percent into seventy-two, you'll find that it takes twelve years for money to double. Conversely, if you know it took a sum twelve years to double you could divide twelve into seventy-two to determine the annual return (6 percent).

SIMPLE INTEREST *(SEE ALSO COMPOUND INTEREST)*—Interest is only earned on the principal balance.

SPLIT ANNUITY—A split annuity is the term given to an effective strategy that utilizes two or more different annuity products—one designed to generate monthly income and the other to restore the original starting principal over a set period of time.

STANDARD & POOR'S 500 (S&P 500)—The most widely used external index by fixed indexed annuities. Its objective is to be a benchmark to measure and report overall U.S. stock market performance. It includes a representative sample of 500 common stocks from companies trading on the New York Stock Exchange, American Stock Exchange, and NASDAQ National Market System. The index represents the price or market value of the underlying stocks and does not include the value of reinvested dividends of the underlying stocks.

STOCK MARKET INDEX—A report created from a type of statistical measurement that shows up or down changes in a specific financial market, usually expressed as points and as a percentage, in a number of related markets, or in an economy as a whole (i.e. S&P 500 or New York Stock Exchange).

SURRENDER CHARGE—A charge imposed for withdrawing funds or terminating an annuity contract prematurely. There is no industry standard for surrender charges; that is, each annuity product has its own unique surrender charge schedule. The charge is usually expressed as a percentage of the amount withdrawn prematurely from the contract. The percentage tends to decline over time, ultimately becoming zero.

TRADITIONAL IRA—*See IRA (Individual Retirement Account)*

TERM END POINT—Crediting methods measuring index movements over a greater timeframe than a year or two. The opposite of an annual reset method. Also referred to as a term point-to point method. Say an index value was at 100 on the first day of the period. If the calculated index value was at 150, at the end of the period the positive index movement would be 50 percent. The company would credit a percentage of this movement as excess interest. Index movement is calculated and interest credited at the end of the term and interim movements during the period are ignored.

TERM HIGH POINT (HIGH WATER MARK)—A type of term end point structure that uses the highest anniversary index level as the end point. Say that the index value was at 100 on the first day of the period, reached a value of 160 at the end of a contract year during the period, and ended the period at 150. A term high point method would use the 160 value—the highest contract anniversary point reached during the period, as the end point and the gross index gain would be 60 percent. The company would then apply a participation rate to the gain.

TERM YIELD SPREAD—A term end point structure that calculates the total index gain for a period computes the annual compound rate of return, deducts a yield spread from the annual rate of return and then recalculates the total index gain for the period based on the net annual rate. Say an index increased from 100 to 200 by the end of a nine-year period. This is the equivalent of an 8 percent compound annual interest rate. If the annuity had a 2 percent term yield spread, this would be deducted from the annual interest rate, and the net rate would be credited to the contract (6 percent), for each of the nine years. Total index gain may also be computed using the highest anniversary index level as the end point.

VARIABLE ANNUITY—A contract issued by an insurance company offering separate accounts invested in a variety of stocks and/or bonds. The investment risk is borne by the annuity owner. Variable annuities are considered securities and require a financial professional to have appropriate securities registration.

1035 EXCHANGE—The 1035 exchange refers to the section of tax code that allows annuity owners the flexibility to exchange one annuity for another without incurring any immediate tax liabilities. This action is most often used when an annuity holder decides they want to upgrade an annuity to a more favorable one, but they do not want to activate unnecessary tax liabilities that would typically be encountered when surrendering an existing annuity contract.

401(K) ROLLOVER—*See IRA Rollover*